<u>Goodbye Social Anxiety</u>

The Only Book on Social Anxiety, Self-Esteem and Self-Confidence You'll Ever Need

David Hamilton & Angelina Williams

Copyright © David Hamilton Publishing

Table of Contents

Prepare To Say Goodbye To Social Anxiety

There are around 15 million people living with social anxiety in America today. Figures gathered from organizations the UK, Australia, and other western European countries also show that anywhere up to 12% of their populations are affected by social phobias, shyness, and anxiety disorders rooted in socialization. This percentage is roughly twice the amount of people suffering from other anxiety conditions. Women and men are equally affected. Experiences with social anxiety can begin during adolescence and span well into adulthood. Sufferers of social anxiety may experience other anxiety disorders or depression at some point in their lives but they may also have no other experiences with mental ill health. People living with social anxiety are just regular people. The person sitting next to you on the bus, your colleagues at work, your nieces and nephews, the guy who sells you your newspaper every morning… any one of these people could be struggling with social discomfort and conversational fear completely unbeknownst to the people around them.

The fact is, symptoms of social anxiety vary greatly from one person to the next. You may find that you are completely petrified by the idea of going out and socializing regardless of the occasion or who's going to be there. Leaving the house at all may fill you with dread just because there's a chance you may run into someone you know and be forced to chat with them. Panic attacks might hold you back from ever leaving the house unless you really have to. But social anxiety isn't always this extreme. You might just feel uncomfortable in social situations. You might find conversing with people face-to-face daunting and awkward. You might struggle to find the right words or act *"normal"* when you're in social situations. Hence, after leaving a conversation with someone you might spend your time thinking back on it and kicking yourself over all the stupid things you said. You might find the idea of a work meeting distressing, or you might obsess about having to attend a large social event for weeks in advance. You may experience anything from mild discomfort to full blown panic attacks.

The good news is that you can cure yourself of social anxiety by simply learning a few new skills. Everyone has the power to change the way they think. All it takes is knowledge and practice. Written in three parts with a variety of practical exercises to help you put theory into practice, this book is going to guide you through methods of thought management that will help you learn to slow down any racing thoughts you may be experiencing, eradicate anxiety for good, and build confidence in the social world.

Part One: Knowledge will help you understand social anxiety more deeply. It will help you find the roots of the anxiety you experience so that you can understand where it comes from and why it has such a hold on you. Unlike other methods which focus on defusing anxiety in the short term, Part One of this book will provide you with a host of long lasting coping skills that you can put into action today and use to eventually conquer social anxiety for good.

Part Two: Practice begins with a section on coping with specific emotionally activating social situations. This is going to give you practical advice on things like dating, meeting new people, attending job interviews, coping with conflict, and running into people you'd rather not be confronted with. Then, sections on how to be a great conversationalist and learning the art of body language will help you build new social skills so that you can feel more confident and make stronger connections with others; thus experiencing genuine satisfaction and enjoyment in the social world. A discussion of life online will tie up this part, highlighting the many unwritten rules and common pitfalls of online socializing.

Part Three: Power is a short section included here to offer you a few final thoughts addressing your self esteem and aiming to give you feelings of empowerment and drive for the future. It will guide you through things like coping with self-doubt, learning to approve of yourself, and the importance of experiencing failure in life. It will encourage you to take everything you have learned in Parts One and Two and use all of it to harness feelings of power, security, inner peace, and self love. Both theoretical and practical advice will help you address your self confidence and fuel you on to reaching for even bigger and better things in life. Finally, you will find a short section on gaining and maintaining healthy relationships. Relationships are a huge part of life. They affect our feelings of confidence and self worth. Unhealthy relationship patterns are often what lies beneath difficulties with depression and anxiety. Learning to eradicate bad relationship patterns and build healthier habits when relating to others is a vital part in any period of self progression.

Before moving on to Part One, I'd like to encourage you to read this book in the order it is written. This book is designed to lead you to complete and total recovery so that you can secure lasting freedom from social anxiety. In life, one cannot jump ahead to Power, without first gaining Knowledge and putting that knowledge into Practice. So, try to resist the urge to jump ahead as you read. Be patient with yourself. Lasting change rarely happens overnight. It takes patience, perseverance, and determination. Make a promise to yourself now to really give yourself a chance to embark on a full journey of recovery rather than seeking a quick fix that's likely to leave you high and dry. You deserve a shot at becoming the person you've always wanted to be. You deserve to be released from the grips of anxiety. You deserve the freedom to be able to walk into a room full of people without feeling awkward or uncomfortable. And you can have all of those things if you accept that it's going to take a little bit of time and effort. I promise you, it will be worth it in the long run.

The Power of Change - Lesson 1

Before moving on, take a moment to think about what your life is like right now. Write down a list of things you are currently struggling with. Write down some things you don't like about your life as it is today. Do not dwell on these negative thoughts or use this exercise to make yourself feel bad about yourself. Rather, just jot a few things down quickly and then put your list away somewhere that you will not be confronted with it again until you choose to be. Think of this as your *"before"* picture. Only when you have completed your journey should you pull this list out of its safe place. At that time, you will be amazed at how far you've come.

Part One: Starting Again

Social Anxiety: What is it and where does it *actually* come from?

Social anxiety is something that can affect virtually anyone. It presents in various ways which can range from basic shyness to full blown agoraphobia and virtually anything in between. You might feel self-conscious in public, nervous about having conversations with people you don't know very well, or you may feel like people are always looking at you or talking about you. You might not want to eat or drink in public, or you may be uncomfortable attending any social events without having a friend at your side. You may feel paranoid about other's perceptions of you, assuming they have negative things to say about you or that they just don't like you. You may have panic attacks in situations like work meetings, riding the bus, or going to theaters or lectures. You may feel overwhelmed or over-stimulated in busy rooms or noisy crowds. You may avoid social situations wherever possible or hold yourself back from personal and professional advancement for fear of failure. The idea of going on a date or attending a job interview might fill you with dread. The list goes on and on. Social anxiety is personal and it affects everyone in different ways. Some people struggle with shyness and anxiety throughout their entire lives. They may have always felt uncomfortable in social spheres due to the role they played in their family growing up, or they may simply be natural introverts. Others may live for decades before social anxiety presents itself, often as a result of a significant life change.

Social anxiety may get worse the longer it goes untreated, similar to other fears and phobias. Someone who experiences their first bout of social anxiety in their early teens for example, may end up struggling with other anxiety disorders, depression, or OCD later in life if they don't have the resources to combat it early on. Someone who has been living with symptoms of anxiety for most of their life may feel hopeless about their future. They may feel like their life is on hold or like things will always be this way. The good news is that social anxiety is something you can get rid of no matter how long it's been a part of your life. Even if it seems like it's a long-term problem, anxiety is still temporary in the grand scheme of things.

There are a variety of circumstances that can cause social anxiety, and thinking about some possible triggers in your own life can help shed some light on why you feel the way you do. For example, if you don't experience extreme symptoms like panic attacks and phobias, but you do feel uncomfortable and awkward when socializing, this may be because you've had limited practice in the social world. Perhaps you were bullied or ostracized when you were growing up. Perhaps one of your parents was overprotective or negligent. Maybe you had a terribly embarrassing experience that continues to haunt you. Or maybe a traumatic event shaped the way you think. Likewise, if social anxiety is something that has fully taken over your life, perhaps you have also lived through bouts of depression or generalized anxiety. Maybe you've experienced difficult relationships with your family or intimate partners. Maybe you've experienced emotional abuse, low self-esteem, or traumatic events that shaped who you are today. A major change in life circumstances such as losing a job, going through a break-up, developing a serious illness, or losing a loved one can also bring about a period of social anxiety. So take some time to think about any events, experiences, or relationships that may have had an effect on your self-confidence or which may have directly caused you to feel anxiety when being around other people. I would caution you against dwelling on negative thoughts when doing this as focussing too much on difficult memories can be counterintuitive to personal development. Try not to use this line of thought in a way that will drag your mood down. But it is important to have an idea about why things have gotten to where they are today. If you feel like social anxiety is just part of who you are, thinking more deeply about where it originated can help combat that negative self belief so that you can maintain hope of living an anxiety-free life. So as you go about your daily life, let your mind wander from time to time into thoughts on the subject. You don't have to sit and write out a long journal entry or even set aside a specific time for this. Just think when it feels natural, like when you're in the shower or when you're cooking. Turn off the TV or radio and leave your cell phone in another room so you can hear your thoughts. Allow them to come in their own time, and when they do just listen to them and let them pass through you. Try not to meet your thoughts with resistance. Really listen to what your inner self is trying to tell you.

It's important to remember that social anxiety acts on a wide spectrum. Not everyone will have specific triggers or traumatic events that got them where they are today. In fact, the apparent rise of social anxiety in the western world over the last few decades could suggest that in fact, certain changes to the way in which we communicate with one another could be causing a change to how we feel when placed in social situations. This presumption is surmounted by the debate that the millennial generation specifically are experiencing higher rates of both social and generalized anxiety than previous generations. If we go down this route of thinking, it could be fair to assume that the relatively newfound popularity of social media and other mobile and internet based communication is having an effect on our ability, as a population, to feel comfortable when communicating with people face-to-face. Of course, ideas like these are being studied and debated by psychologists and social thinkers worldwide with varying results, so it would be naive to place too much weight here. Doing so could mean ignoring the experiences of individuals in favor of judging society as a whole. However, keep this in mind as you think about your own presentations of social anxiety.

Is it possible that your cell phone has a hand in the anxiety you're experiencing?

Do you feel more comfortable when communicating with people via text or email than you do in person?
Do you use social media as your main form of socializing and conversing with others?
Do you experience anxiety or lowered self esteem as a direct result of spending time perusing social media?
Do you judge yourself harshly when viewing the way other people present their lives online?
Do you use text based communication as a way of avoiding socializing in real life?

This is a topic I will return to later, but keep this thought alive as you move through your daily life. Think about how much you use technology instead of conversing face-to-face or even talking to people over the phone. Try to assess if using social media is having a negative effect on your psyche. Always be honest and realistic with yourself when thinking like this.

Living with anxiety of any variety isn't easy. Many people living with social anxiety also experience generalized anxiety or panic disorder and may also experience increased periods of low mood and depression. The fact is, living with anxiety is tiring. Anxious thoughts are chaotic and fast paced. Worry creates a frenzied way of thinking, especially when it's irrational. When anxiety has a hold on you, your thoughts are likely to be obsessive and cyclical. You may go over the same *"what-ifs"* again and again. You may visualize a scene going wrong in a hundred different ways. You may catapult yourself into worst case scenarios before, during, and after important meetings and social events. This means feeling drained, exasperated, and emotionally exhausted. You might not be able to sleep well at night or you may want to sleep all the time. Fatigue is common among anxiety sufferers and it's easy to see why!

Plus, the more we get swept away in racing thoughts, the harder it becomes to see clearly and think rationally. When anxiety has a hold on you, it's hard to remember what life was like before. It's hard to imagine life without harmful racing thoughts badgering you all the time. It's hard to believe that you still have the possibility to overcome the way things are now and find yourself in a contented, peaceful future.

Anxiety is very good at holding us back. It keeps us rooted to the spot. It makes us believe that this is just the way things are and we will never be able to escape its grip. But take solace in the fact that those beliefs are simply not true. The thing is, anxiety is addictive and habitual. Harmful thought patterns, irrational self-beliefs, and interpreting neutral or even positive situations as negative can be addictive behavior. People aren't born as optimists and pessimists. What we take from situations in life usually reflects the way we think and feel at any given moment. If we are used to feeling anxious, we're more likely to harness negative feelings about ourselves and the world around us. Hence, we may leave a conversation and obsess over everything we said that could've made us sound stupid rather than remembering any of the things we said that were actually witty and intelligent.

Similarly, if you get panic attacks every time you get on the bus or the train, you may find that the anxiety itself is the real trigger. The anxiety is an addiction that is linked to a certain activity. It is not that the activity itself has become more dangerous or threatening than it was before you began experiencing panic attacks. It's that after one panic attack, you're more likely to have another. And after twenty panic attacks, you're likely to have thirty more. Like any habit or addiction, the more you give into anxiety, the stronger it becomes. The more power you give it, the weaker you are when it comes to stealing that power away from it. Every time you avoid a trigger, you are giving anxiety the power. After all, it's rarely the bus that someone's really afraid of deep down. The fact is that panic attacks themselves are terrifying. So it's natural to want to avoid anything that might bring one on. But avoidance and addiction are a dangerous combination. It will take determination, practice, and repetition to break unhelpful cycles and start slowly moving out of your comfort zone. That is why this book focuses on lasting techniques to address and obliterate your anxiety for good. There is no point in putting a band-aid on a broken arm. Therefore, using methods that only work *"in the moment"* is not going to give you a lasting solution. The road to a full recovery may be a little bit longer and it will take work, but if you have the possibility to release yourself from anxiety for good and completely regain power over your life, why wouldn't you?

At this point, I'm going to say something that I really want you to hear. Anxiety is not part of who you are. It is not part of your identity. When we believe that anxiety - or any other difficulties on the mental health spectrum - are part of our identity, we are robbing ourselves of hope. Think about it. How can anyone be hopeful of change and a more positive peaceful future if they believe that this is just the way things are and how they will always be? It would be impossible to hold out any amount of hope if anxiety was thought of as fixed or permanent. Therefore, I would suggest that you be careful about how you choose to speak of anxiety. There is danger in referring to anxiety in a possessive manner. If you've ever heard yourself using the phrase, *"my* anxiety"*, think about what subconscious message that phrase is actually saying. For example, listen to this sentence and try to identify what's wrong with it: *"I'm sorry, I'm not going to be able to make it out tonight. I'm having a hard time with my anxiety right now."*

Can you see what negative self belief the phrase *"my* anxiety" may be subliminally suggesting to you? The word "my" suggests *ownership*. It suggests a level of ownership that is solid and unchangeable. If I talk to you about "my eyes" or "my stomach", would you question whether or not these things belong to me? Of course you wouldn't, and I don't either. My eyes and my stomach are mine. They are a part of me and this is not debatable. So by the same rite, if you speak of anxiety as though it belongs to you, you are telling yourself that this fact is not debatable. You are telling yourself that this is an integral part of your identity; one that cannot be separated from you. But the more you believe that anxiety is part of your identity, the more skewed your self beliefs may become. You may develop a poor self image and feel hopeless about ever having a future absent of anxiety. In order to grow past anxiety, and live up to our true potential we have to be free to view ourselves as strong and capable. You may be affected by something difficult right now, but that struggle does not have to be part of who you are. If you often take ownership of social anxiety by using phrases like "my anxiety", try to break that habit. Do not own anxiety. Do not claim it as part of you. This is going to be hard if you've lived with anxiety for a long time.

Remembering who you were before it might be difficult. Picturing who you will be *after* anxiety could be even harder. But it's important to start creating a healthier self image for yourself now. One that is stable, truthful, and hopeful. You have eyes and you have a stomach, but anxiety is just something you're experiencing. It is changeable. You have undoubtedly suffered from a cold or flu in the past, right? Perhaps you broke a limb and had to wear a cast for a couple of months. Maybe you cut your finger and needed stitches. Were these things ever allowed to become part of your identity? Were they then, or are they now, a part of who you are? No. They were just things you experienced. They were things that affected you at one time. But now, they are just memories. You may have a scar or two, but you are not still that person with a broken limb. You are not a cold or a flu. You are not a person who will have stitches for the rest of your life.

This is how I want you to think of anxiety. It is not a part of you and it never has been a part of you, even if it feels like it has been. It is just something you have experienced and continue to experience in your life as it is today. But no matter how long you have been experiencing it, you can be free of it. Soon it will pass. You will go through a journey of self development and eventually be on the other side of it. You may have a scar or two, but you will not be forever moulded by it.

How To Let Go, Fast

If we take a broad view of anxiety, we can assert that the things we generally find to be the most difficult to cope with are those which are out of our control. If we face a conflict with a straightforward solution, we are unlikely to become anxious about the issue. Chances are, we'll assess the problem and carry out a solution until it is resolved. However, the more complicated a problem is, and the less control we have over the outcome, the more anxiety is likely to creep up. Again, taking a broad view of anxiety and life as a whole, this is problematic. The fact is, life is chaotic and unpredictable by nature. If we weigh out the things we can control versus the things we cannot control, each one of us is at a gross disadvantage. Even when life is going well, it only takes a second for things to spontaneously come crashing down all around us. People get sick. Accidents happen. Jobs are lost. Relationships end. Betrayals occur. None of us have control over unforeseen forces. None of us can predict spontaneous disruption to our lives. This can be a very unsettling thought. Someone who experiences generalized anxiety disorder for instance, could be dangerously preoccupied with myriad things that could possibly go wrong in any given moment. And that makes sense. It's hard for the human brain to cope with its lack of control over its surroundings. Having a sense of control breeds feelings of security, stability, and predictability. Where that control is absent, worry worms its way in.

For the purpose of this book, let's call this facet of the human condition *"chaos based anxiety"*; that is to say, anxiety which is rooted in that which we cannot control. Now let's narrow our broad view down a bit and think of the idea of chaos based anxiety where *social* anxiety is concerned. Most people living with social anxiety have a tendency to try to predict the future, often subconsciously. They consider attending social events and can't help imagining everything that could possibly go wrong. They envision upcoming conversations and naturally see them in a negative light. They see themselves making idiotic social faux pas, saying the wrong thing, or coming across as socially awkward. They imagine having a panic attack and having to get up and leave a room that is otherwise silent. They picture themselves having a terrible time. And in order to gain a sense of control over this social event they're still only considering attending, they might spend time trying to think of what to say if a certain topic comes up. They try to plan how they will react if they run into someone they don't want to see. They may imagine themself as an outsider in a room full of people having a good time. They may picture themself nervous and uncomfortable, spending the whole time sitting by the door staring at the clock until they can finally go home. They imagine a bunch of different scenarios which may or may not happen and obsess about how they'll handle them if they do.

Someone who experiences panic attacks on public transport or during work meetings will often start to panic before they're even in their trigger environment because they are already *predicting* the inevitability of the attack. The point is, the instinct to try to predict what's going to happen in any given situation is a natural response to having no control over it. Whether your thoughts are relentless or more subdued, anxiety loves situations that lack control and predictability. The instinct to try to predict the future is particularly strong if someone has recently been experiencing social discomfort. Memories of awkward encounters and things that went wrong often make their way into the psyche around this time too, making the need for control even greater. So it makes sense that people living in the grips of anxiety would consciously or subconsciously try to get a hold of the situation at hand. The unfortunate thing is that attempting to predict or control things that are completely out of our hands is not just a wasted effort, it's also serving to *increase* feelings of anxiety.

Instead of allowing ourselves to worry about what is going to happen in a social situation, we have to learn to let go and go with the flow, and this takes practice. You cannot possibly prepare for every possible outcome, and allowing yourself to indulge in that way of thinking is only going to increase the anxiety you're feeling. The more you focus on the possibilities of what can go wrong, the more you are inadvertently working yourself up. The more you imagine all the different ways a conversation may go, the more you are reminding yourself that you have limited control over the situation, thus adding fuel to anxiety's fire. Try to remember that the antidote to chaos and unpredictability is *not* gaining control and a sense of predictability.

Rather, the antidote to chaos and unpredictability is gaining acceptance and a willingness to wait and see. None of us will ever be able to control life's chaos. All we can do is learn to accept it, let go, and stop indulging in *"what ifs"*. We have to embrace our own powerlessness so that we can feel comfortable in the confines of worries that would otherwise derail us.

Now I know this may sound reductive and I assure you, I am not trying to minimize how intensely anxiety may be affecting you. Getting rid of obsessive thoughts and negative thought patterns is no easy feat. But believe it or not, the one thing you can gain control over is how you think. If you learn how to slow down your thinking and employ rational thought processes to combat harmful thought patterns, eventually you will gain control over the way you think. And once you have control of the way you think, you will have control over anxiety. So I am not attempting to minimize the effect that anxiety is having on you, but rather I am suggesting that you begin regularly checking in with yourself about what's going on in your thought processes. When you feel anxiety rising, start asking yourself if you're overthinking something or attempting to predict the future. If the answer is yes, tell yourself to stop. Recognize when you have no control over a situation and try to embrace it. Rationalize your *"what ifs"* by asking yourself questions to counteract them.

If you attend a social event and things actually do go horribly wrong, so what?
Is that occurrence going to have a lasting effect on your life?

Even if something really embarrassing happens to you, is anyone else even going to remember it or care about it at all?

Will you be forever affected by it or will you take some time to lick your wounds and eventually bounce back?

Will you still care about this next year?

Are you the only person who has ever done something stupid or embarrassing?

How would you treat a friend who was in the same situation? Would you judge them and laugh at them? No. Chances are you'd offer some compassion and encouragement and then you'd forget about it in a few days.

Questioning yourself like this and creating this type of inner dialogue is very important in thought management. We have to be able to talk ourselves off that ledge when anxiety tries to push us closer to it. Rational thinking and gaining perspective is the most powerful tool you can wield over anxiety. It is the type of thing that can cut through irrational thinking and emotions that are rooted in fear. Learning to control your thoughts is a skill that will only get stronger with practice, so try to employ slow, logical thinking as often as you possibly can. When dealing with anxiety, you are essentially trying to rewrite the way you perceive and think about things, so it will take repetition. Every time you recognize that your thoughts are veering into dangerous territory, use logical questions and rational thinking to cut through harmful thoughts. Then tell yourself, *"This worry is a waste of my time. It is accomplishing nothing other than making me feel bad. There is no point in worrying about something that is completely out of my control."*

Then let go of that worry. If it creeps back up, repeat the process. Do it as many times as you have to. The more practice you get, the better. You will soon notice that it doesn't take as long for you to slow things down and get perspective. When it comes to thought management, practice makes perfect.

Often times, anxiety that is centered around social situations is dominated by a fear of rejection. This can be conscious or subconscious and can be the case for many reasons. For example, a person who grew up with parents that never approved of them or who neglected to give them attention or praise, may struggle with feelings of inferiority. They may have a hard time approving of themselves and may be particularly sensitive to rejection. Feeling as though a friend, colleague, or partner is critical or disapproving of them could cause feelings as severe devastation and self-loathing.

Similarly, harmful or emotionally abusive relationship patterns can also lead to feelings of low self-worth which can lead to a fear of rejection. A recent change to one's circumstances can also affect the way they view themselves in the world around them. Losing a job, going through a divorce, making a serious mistake, or struggling with substance abuse can also lead to heightened feelings of shame and fear of rejection. Feeling trapped in situations you cannot change may also factor into social anxiety. For instance, if you're unhappy at work but you've been unsuccessful at finding a new job, your self-esteem may plummet. A fear of having to endure rejection in other parts of your life could arise. There are, as you can see, countless reasons one might develop a fear of rejection or disapproval. Low self-esteem, self-loathing, and poor self-image often result from comparing ourselves to other people; putting them on a pedestal and ourselves nearly underground.

The problem is that if we're living with fear of rejection as an undercurrent to our lives, it's only natural that we will eventually start to view the social world with trepidation. Disruptions to our self-image do not make socializing any easier. And if we add in the possibility of being judged harshly or being viewed in a negative light by others, it's only natural that we'll start to feel uncomfortable in social situations. But just as we have to learn to let go of worry, so do we need to let go of this fear of not being accepted by others. It is true that human beings have a fundamental need to belong in social groups. We are social beings by nature. Belonging to something bigger than ourselves is important when it comes to maintaining feelings of positive self-worth and emotional security. But in order to achieve this, we first have to accept that rejection is a part of life. It is not necessarily a reflection of who we are or what we're worth. None of us can successfully belong to every social group we come across. We are all too unique for that to be the case. We have to be okay with the fact that some people aren't going to like us, because there are also going to be people that we don't like in return.

Not all prospective lovers are going to be the right fit. Not all friend groups are going to invite us in with open arms. Most of us will be excluded from cliques in work and at school. This is also the nature of being pack animals. Sometimes it takes a while to find your pack. When we are able to accept that rejection is a natural human struggle - something we *all* experience throughout our lives - we can take some of the sting out of it. Furthermore, by learning to approve of ourselves, rather than relying on the approval and admiration of others to dictate our worth, we can grow a thicker skin in the face of adversity. Our self-worth and self-esteem will not be in the hands of those who don't deserve it.

There is nothing more powerful than self-approval. There is no greater gift we can give ourselves than our own love and praise. We have to take the time to recognize our strengths, to pat ourselves on the back when we've done a good job. We have to praise ourselves when we've accomplished something, no matter how small. So what if we didn't get the job? At least we put ourselves out there and gave it a try. That took courage. So what if we had to leave a social event because of a panic attack. The fact that we showed up at all was an accomplishment. We have to judge ourselves realistically and compassionately, not focus on all the things we could've or should've done better. We have to be our own cheerleaders, because no one else is obligated to do that for us. Most importantly, we have to live a life we can be proud of. We have to live up to our own morals and standards. We need to recognize where changes need to be made. Make apologies when we owe them. Then forgive ourselves and move on. No holding onto past mistakes in order to make ourselves feel bad.

No reminding ourselves of past embarrassments in order to hold ourselves back from going out and enjoying our lives. No telling ourselves that we're not good enough. We have to learn to see the good in ourselves and see that we all deserve happiness in life. We all deserve a sense of inner peace.

So if you are holding onto memories of past embarrassments and using them to hurt yourself or to kick yourself when you're down, try to let them go. What happened in the past is gone now, be done with it. If you're holding onto the memory of a bad relationship as an excuse to avoid meeting new people, stop holding yourself back and let that go. Your past does not dictate your future. If you're afraid of trying new things or making mistakes because you're still hurting over something you wish you'd done better, let it go. If we all held onto every mistake we ever made, self love wouldn't even be a concept let alone a reality. If you're holding onto irrational fears and worries, let them go. They are not serving you. Whatever it is that's clinging to you and keeping you held hostage in social anxiety, make a promise to yourself to figure out what it is, address it, and let it go. Don't let life pass you by over anxiety. You can beat anxiety. Anyone can.

The Power of Change – Lesson 2

Take a moment now to set some goals for yourself. Think about what it is you'd like to achieve during this journey. These can be things as specific as wanting to be able to face a certain trigger without experiencing anxiety or they can be more broad such as wanting to love yourself more or achieve a greater sense of overall happiness. Write down as much as you like.

The rules are: *be realistic and optimistic.*

Think about where you would like to be in 2 weeks… then 2 months… a year.
What hurdles do you want to overcome?

What things have you been avoiding that you'd like to finally conquer?
What do you want your life to look like in the future?
In what ways would you like to improve yourself?

Hold onto your list and refer to it anytime your motivation wanes. Remember that self-progression often involves setbacks. You will need the strength to get back up after a fall. Having this list close by could help you bounce back more quickly if things veer a little off track.

Coping Skills That Work and Keep Working

When it comes to coping with anxiety, there is no point indulging in strategies that will only offer relief in the short term. Let's face it, even if you've only been dealing with anxiety for a month or so, you've probably had enough of it by now. You're probably ready to send it packing. Plus, it's possible that the longer you live with anxiety, the harder it can be to get rid of it. Therefore, it is important that when you are fighting anxiety, you are using tools and techniques; ones that are going to give you lasting results. What's the point in gaining short term relief in one moment if anxiety is going to rear its ugly head again in the next? The fact is, by changing the way you think and how you perceive the world around you, in addition to building healthy habits of self-approval and self-care, you can be free of anxiety for good. All you need is determination, resilience, and the right tools. Let's be honest there's no use bringing a slingshot if you're going to war.

So what exactly am I referring to when I talk about unhelpful short term fixes? There are a number of techniques people use to cope with anxiety that offer relief yet aren't helpful in the long run. In fact, many of them actually serve to make anxiety worse the more dependent you become on them. In your journey so far, you may have come across things like counting techniques wherein you do something such as counting down backwards from 100 in multiples of 3. Others focus on naming things like animals from A-Z, or baby names from Z-A. These techniques are designed to be used in moments of severe anxiety or panic, and I am not disputing their efficacy. It's true that exercises like this can help to defuse a panic attack. They can distract you from your anxiety long enough to get you through a heightened period.

However, using techniques like this too often and over a significant period of time will not lead to lasting relief because they are subconsciously sending you the wrong message. Rather than addressing the problem beneath the anxiety, they simply address what lies on the surface. That's why you can use these types of techniques again and again and still experience panic and anxiety resulting from the same exact triggers. By seeking to distract you rather than helping you think more slowly and clearly, exercises like this are telling you that there actually *is* something to fear.

They are reiterating the thoughts and feelings that caused the anxiety to spike in the first place. By leading you to simply look away from anxiety instead of seeking to understand it, these techniques are telling you that the fear you're experiencing is real and justified. Distracting yourself from a fear is the exact opposite of facing and dismantling it. Doing so subconsciously tells yourself that not only is there something to fear, but also that it is so scary the only thing you can do to deal with it is look away. Thus, it is taking the power away from you and placing it in fear's hands. It's like sleeping with the lights on because you're afraid of the dark. Or never going on vacation because you're afraid to fly. Sure, plenty of people live their lives giving into fear on a regular basis, but in doing so, they are limiting their experience and enjoyment of life by placing unnecessary restrictions on themselves. They are giving into irrational fears instead of facing them. But please remember: Anxiety is not harmful enough to sign your life away to it. It does not have to be a permanent feature in your life. You just have to accept that anxiety isn't something you can hide from forever and expect it to magically go away one day. You have to actively take the power back. You have to be able to look anxiety in the face, understand it and overpower it. No matter how powerful a force it may be in your life right now, anyone can gain power over anxiety.

Fear plays a significant role in human survival. It is the instinct that keeps us safe when we face potential danger. It is a vital part of self-protection and safety. But when allowed to run wild, fear can dominate our minds. It can cause us to misinterpret situations, to view them as dangerous or threatening when in fact, they are not. It can cause us to view potential social missteps as catastrophic. It can cause us to place too much emphasis on insignificant communications and events. Anxiety loves to make you think there is something to fear when there isn't. So instead of agreeing that there is something to fear and closing our eyes to do some counting techniques and measured breathing, we have to accept that the fear we are experiencing is irrational and instead, employ slow, logical, realistic thinking to cut through it. We have to look at the situation, assess it realistically, and defuse harmful racing thoughts. The more often we do this, the better we will become at controlling our thought processes, and the stronger we will be the next time anxiety creeps up. It's a method that simply cannot be argued with, because it really works, and it works for good. This type of skill - the skill of *thought management* - is something that never goes away. It only gets stronger the more you continue to use and perfect it. It can never be undone or unlearned.

Every time you use slow, logical thinking to defuse anxiety, you are honing this skill. You will feel bigger and stronger, while anxiety begins to appear smaller and weaker. Each time you face anxiety, you will notice that the speed at which you can calm yourself down will get faster and faster. Eventually you'll notice that an occurrence that would have taken an hour to get through in the past, will take just a few moments to navigate. Anxiety that would've hung around like a bad smell will dissipate just moments after you detect it. And the best part is that there is no "square one" in self progression. Slips and setbacks happen to everyone; we all have bad days and it's wise to be realistic about that; but once you've put in the work, it will always be there. Once you've retrained the way you think, it will never go back to how it used to be. Once you've won the fight against anxiety, and you've perfected the skill of thought management, you will be cured of it.

Now, I know that in theory this all sounds very good but where do you start? You may be skeptical of your capabilities. You may worry that even if you take the time to understand anxiety, you still won't be able to shake it, especially if you've suffered with anxiety or depression in the past or you've been living with it for an extended period of time. Try not to doubt yourself at this stage. Hold onto hope and trust that by simply purchasing this book you have proven that you are ready for a change. You have to start somewhere, and identifying unhelpful coping techniques is a strong way to get moving. If you are currently experiencing severe anxiety or panic attacks, it is natural to want to cling to your old coping habits, and I will not be encouraging you to try to change these things overnight. Slow and steady wins the race. If you always carry a bottle of water with you and use distraction techniques when you're feeling challenged, it's going to take a lot of courage to break that cycle. You probably won't be able to do it right away. Long term coping techniques do take more work. Retraining your thought processes takes practice and perseverance. Doing this gradually isn't going to be a *quick fix*, but it will be a *permanent fix*. So ask yourself now, do you want to keep patching up that hole in your psyche where anxiety lives? Or would you rather build a wall that it will never be able to penetrate again? Do you value yourself and your life enough to put in some work that will end this problem for good? The answer to this question has to be YES.

Before you can build all new coping skills, you'll need to start by assessing your current ways of coping with anxiety. Take some time to think about what you are doing to cope before, during, and after situations that cause a rise in nervousness or emotional activation. Be as honest with yourself as you can. Remember that this is your journey, you are in charge. But if you're not honest with yourself, you'll only hold yourself back.

Are you currently avoiding social situations?
If so, are you avoiding all social situations or just ones that are new or particularly daunting?

Do you avoid meeting new people or going to events in places that you are unfamiliar with?
If you experience panic attacks, are you changing the way you do things in an attempt to avoid triggers?
For instance, do you avoid public transport or insist on sitting near the door or bathroom when you're in social situations?

Do you use alcohol or drugs to make socializing easier?
Do you cancel plans with friends regularly?
Do you use counting techniques to calm yourself when anxiety spikes?
Do you cling to your cell phone or a friend when you're uncomfortable?
Do you choose to socialize online instead of in person?
Do you experience anxiety for days at a time in anticipation of upcoming emotionally activating circumstances?
If so, is there anything you are currently doing that effectively calms you down during this time?

Is there something you're doing that is helping in the short term but not fully stopping anxiety in its tracks?

Once you have a good grasp on your current coping mechanisms, it's time to start challenging them. Even if you feel like some of your techniques are helping to make things easier on you, be honest with yourself about how long they actually work. Would you have purchased this book if your current techniques were having a lasting effect? Probably not. Has the magnitude of your anxiety lessened at all since starting to use short term techniques or has it actually only increased? At this stage, it's time to start taking some baby steps towards letting go of coping mechanisms that are getting you nowhere. Sometimes, we have to scrap everything and just start again. Just remember that it's okay to move slowly with things like this. Trying to do too much too soon could have an adverse effect. The aim is to become aware of any current behaviors that aren't helping, and begin to replace them with ones that will. Remember to be realistic with your expectations. No one goes through a period of personal growth without experiencing some setbacks and challenges, so please do not use these incidents as an excuse to give up. This is going to work but it might not be easy. When you fall, get back up and try again. That's all there is for it.

Now is a good time to start using active logical thinking as an antidote to anxiety. This means looking at each emotionally activating situation with a clear head in order to combat irrational negative emotions and catastrophic thoughts. This is something you should do before, during, and after situations that make you uncomfortable. Most people attempt to do this to some extent when anxiety gets the better of them but if you do it often enough, at every stage of emotional activation, while letting go of any unhelpful coping skills you've been using up to now, you will start implementing lasting change.

Here's how it works:
(1) Preempting anxiety by thinking clearly *before* you are likely to become anxious, you can dramatically lessen the extent to which anxiety affects you while giving yourself more courage when facing anxiety-inducing situations in the future. If you can predict a moment of anxiety before it strikes, you may be able to prevent it from knocking you down by keeping your thoughts in healthy territory. If you anticipate a wave of anxiety before it strikes, you can think clearly about why you might feel anxious and use logical thinking to stop it before it gains steam.

(2) Using slow, logical thinking to defuse full blown anxiety *in the moment* will reduce the amount of time you are affected by it.

This means being able to cut through anxiety with relative ease and move on rather than letting your whole day be dominated by it. You will not only give yourself freedom from harmful thought patterns, but also the ability to remain in anxiety-inducing situations and even begin to enjoy yourself. Being able to shake off anxiety when it's at its peak means you will be able to move on from it quickly and build strength against it in the long run.

(3) Reflecting on an emotionally activating situation *after it has passed* will give you a chance to consider what forces triggered your feelings of anxiety and discomfort. Understanding why things became difficult for you is a big part of gaining power over anxiety, so it can be smart to try to unpack any feelings that may have contributed to your negative experience. Reflection is also extremely important for you to be able to mark any progress you've made, recognize and praise yourself for any improvements you've made where coping mechanisms are concerned, and think about which techniques helped to reduce the anxiety and which did not.

This is an ideal time to consider how things went as well as assessing how you can do even better the next time. Self-praise and self-approval are very important parts of self-progression, so it's important to take time to reflect on things after the fact. Being able to spot any improvements you've made, no matter how small, gives you a chance to feel good about all the hard work you're putting into yourself. Reflection is all about gaining knowledge, and gaining knowledge is the key to gaining power. Get used to thinking actively about situations after they've occurred and be prepared to use that knowledge to fuel yourself on rather than to hold yourself back.

Whenever you begin to feel nervous, worried, or anxious, make a resolve to stop and think clearly about the situation at hand. Look at it realistically. Take emotion and irrationality out of the picture. The more often you take time to actively think like this, with the clearest mind you possibly can, the more natural this way of thinking will become. Eventually you will not have to remind yourself to slow things down or think with a more realistic view. Rather, slow, logical thinking will naturally replace harmful, racing thoughts. It will simply become your default way of thinking. You will be able to manage your thoughts so effectively that anxiety will rarely appear at all anymore. The most important part of using rational thinking against anxiety is that you must continue to think slowly and logically until you feel yourself calming down. If you rate the anxiety from 1 to 10 when you feel it spiking, you have to encourage yourself think slowly and clearly while remaining in the anxiety-provoking situation until that anxiety rating drops.

For example, let's say you arrive at a busy bar and you rate the anxiety at an 8. If you leave while the rating is this high, you are inadvertently telling yourself that there *is* something to fear and that the only thing you can do to save yourself is to get out of the situation. This means that the next time you are confronted with a similar situation, the anxiety rating is likely to be the same or even higher. The more we avoid situations or leave when we're in a heightened state, the more we grow to believe that we can't exist comfortably in those surroundings.

Conversely, if you slow your thinking down and begin to think logically and clearly while staying right where you are, that anxiety rating will eventually begin to drop. The longer you stay in the situation, the more you are proving to yourself that your fears are irrational. By staying in that situation until the anxiety rating is below 5, or ideally below 3, you are proving to yourself that there is nothing to fear and that there is no reason to flee the scene. During this type of staying exercise, you are gaining strength and anxiety is getting weaker. Remaining in anxiety-inducing situations until you begin to feel better is something I will return to many times throughout this book as it is the most effective way to face social fears, get rid of social anxiety and panic attacks, and regain comfort and enjoyability in social situations.

Real Life Coping Skills

Asking yourself questions is one of the easiest and most effective ways to slow down unhelpful racing thoughts. It serves to bring in a second inner voice - one that can stand up to your harmful primary inner voice - one that is working *for you* and *against anxiety*. Imagine your inner self split in two: your primary self-experiences anxiety in all sorts of situations regardless of whether or not any true danger is present, while your secondary self perceives the world rationally and realistically. The aim is to move your rational self into the primary position by using thought management to employ slow, logical, realistic thinking *all the time*. Here's what this type of thinking looks like. Note how inquisitive and curious these voices are. Note how they are designed to cut through irrationality and provide a more realistic view of a situation:

(1) How important is this conversation or event really?
Why have I built this up so much in my head?
Is this still going to have any significant effect on me?
Will I still be bothered about it by next week or next year?
Is anyone else who is involved in this event considering it to be as big a deal as I am?
Is anyone else this worked up over this particular situation?
If not, is this really worth so much of my energy?
Am I taking this all a little too seriously?

(2) What is really going to happen if this all goes horribly wrong or something embarrassing happens to me in public?
What will happen if I say something stupid or if I trip and fall? I may feel embarrassed.
Have I felt embarrassed before? *Yes.*
Did I survive? *Yes.*
Does everyone make mistakes and feel embarrassed sometimes? *Yes.*

If this particular embarrassment happened to someone else would
I put them down or judge them over it? *No.* I would feel
compassion and empathy for them.
Do I deserve my own compassion and empathy? *Yes.*
If something embarrassing does happen to me, is anyone else
going to remember it as much as I am? *No.* They probably won't
even notice me and if they do, they'll probably feel compassion
and empathy and then they will forget about it.

At this stage, is there any point in getting worked up over
something that hasn't even happened yet? No. If something
unfortunate happens, I'll shake it off and get over it. Imagining
worst case scenarios is not going to help me cope with anxiety
right now.

(3) I have a specific fear of being so nervous that I throw up in
public. This is something that gets worse with panic attacks and
it's especially bad when I'm talking to someone face-to-face. I
become preoccupied with feeling nauseous and can't even focus
on what the other person is saying.

Is this actually a realistic fear? *No.* If it was, no one would ever
talk face-to-face with anyone!

Have I ever actually been sick in a situation like this? *No.* I have
felt like I might be sick a hundred times but it has never actually
happened.

If I did actually get sick what would happen? I'd probably excuse
myself and get to the bathroom in time. I might feel awkward and
embarrassed but I'd probably be the only person thinking of it in a
negative light. Where I am at this moment, can I get to the
bathroom if I really need to? *Yes.*

Do I really need to sit directly beside the bathroom or can I trust that I'll get there if I really need to? *No* I don't need to sit by the bathroom just because I'm scared of something that's probably not going to happen. I'm a grown up, I can get to the bathroom regardless of where I sit.

Is anyone going to think twice if I need to excuse myself to go to the bathroom? *No!*

How would other people react if I were to actually get sick in public? They would feel sorry for me. Someone would probably offer help. I'd be embarrassed but I'd survive.

How can I stop thinking about being sick when I'm trying to have a conversation with someone? I can relax since I know where the bathroom is should I need it. I can recognize that although I have felt sick on many occasions, I have never spontaneously been sick in public.

How can I shift my focus away from how I'm feeling physically? I can focus on the other person and really listen to what they're saying instead of listening to my own unhelpful thoughts. I can ask them questions and show that I'm interested in what they are saying. I can focus on trying to enjoy myself.

(4) I'm in a busy room and feel like I'm on display.

Is anyone in this room actually looking at me right now? Do any of them really care about how I look or what I say? *No.* Everyone else in this room is completely preoccupied with how *they* look and what *they* say. Most of these people will leave here and forget about everything that happened other than how they came across to other people. People are naturally self-focused. They are not looking at me or judging me. They are thinking about themselves the same way I'm thinking about myself.

If someone actually is looking at me or judging me, does that person have some kind of power over me? Is what they think of me really that important? Not really. It's not pleasant to be thought of negatively but what other people think of me is none of my business.

These are just some examples of how to defuse unhelpful thought patterns and challenge false beliefs that may arise in social situations. Your inner voice will of course, be tailored to your own current limitations and self-beliefs. Just think of it as listening to your concerns and talking to yourself like you would talk to a friend. In a moment of anxiety, you have to be patient with yourself and treat yourself with kindness. It is often much easier to speak to other people this way than it is to do so with ourselves. Many of us are used to putting ourselves down or only seeing the ways we're falling short. We rarely take time to praise ourselves when we overcome difficulties and we rarely take the time to think slowly and be gentle with ourselves.

If you have a hard time being kind to yourself, just imagine that you are talking to a friend.

What would you say to someone who was feeling anxious?
What would you say if you knew that they were focusing on unlikely and *unhelpful "what ifs"* and that in doing so, they were giving in to irrational thoughts?
What if you could see clearly when they couldn't?
Would you beat them up for having irrational fears and getting swept up in anxiety?
Or would you be understanding and seek to help them gain clarity and courage instead?
How would you help them get perspective?

A big part of anxiety is being able to see clearly, to look at the bigger picture and use it as a weapon against the narrow view anxiety is causing. This way you can effectively minimize the magnitude of the anxiety while making yourself feel stronger and more capable of overcoming it. When you have reached the end of an emotionally activating situation, do not think about all the things you could've done better. Don't put yourself down for feeling anxious over something so insignificant. Instead, be good to yourself. Recognize that you are attempting to break a habit and that it's going to take some time and a lot of trial and error before you have complete control over it. If your inner dialogue is negative, make a resolve turn it around. Take note of the things you handled better than you would have in the past, no matter how small the advancement. Give yourself a pat on the back for enduring the situation rather than being mad at yourself for being overly-sensitive. As you already know, self-praise and self-approval are extremely important. We have to be able to recognize every single time we make an improvement, no matter how small it may seem at the time.

We have to recognize when we're doing something to positively impact our lives. Because things like this aren't easy. Remember that rejection and a need for approval are often sitting at the foundation of social anxiety. Slowing your thinking down will help you address the anxiety more effectively, but you also need to make sure that your foundation is solid and stable. Reflecting on anxiety-inducing situations after the fact and giving yourself recognition for getting through them is vital for building that strong foundation. So treat yourself just like you would treat a friend. Don't pick out all the things you could've done better. Instead, focus on the ways in which you improved and let yourself feel good about them. You can always make more improvements next time. Moments of praise and reward are of equal importance to retraining your thought processes, so it's important to take this seriously. For now, have a look at the following list which offers 7 healthy, long lasting ways to deal with social anxiety and get rid of it for good.

7 Long Lasting Coping Skills

<u>**1 - Practice daily self-care.**</u>
In today's world, we hear people talk about self-care quite a lot, and this is an incredibly positive change for society as a whole. Just a few years ago, the words *"self-care"* were rarely uttered. Nowadays they are much more recognizable but may still be fairly mysterious in meaning. What does exercising good self-care really mean?

Self-care is defined by activities that are done purely for one's own enjoyment and wellbeing. It is something that will vary from person to person and it is hugely important for emotional maintenance. It is an effective way to *prevent* surges of anxiety and can even be used to treat an acute moment of anxiety or panic. Self-care is the emotional equivalent of oxygen, food, and water for the physical self. If we neglect to take care of our emotional selves, it is only natural that feelings of anxiety, stress, depression, and low self-confidence may follow. In order for the emotional self to be strong and resilient, we have to give it the attention it deserves. Every time we do something nice for ourselves, we are telling ourselves that we love and approve of the person we are. We are battling feelings of self-loathing and low self-esteem. We are giving ourselves the kindness and support we find so much easier to offer to other people. And likewise, every time we neglect our emotional selves, and starve them of the care they require, we are telling ourselves that we are not worthy of love or approval. We are putting ourselves last on our list of priorities. During a period of self-progression, we cannot afford to live on bare minimums.

Self-care is something you should be actively doing every single day. If you're not sure where to start, begin by writing a list of things you like doing just for yourself. These shouldn't be things that involve multi-tasking, getting things done, or taking care of other people. However, they don't necessarily have to be solitary acts. Some examples of self-care include taking a bath, walking in a scenic area, playing with your dog, going for a long drive, attending yoga or meditation classes, exercising, giving yourself a facial, meeting up with friend who affects you positively, playing a game with your kids, or exercising your creativity by painting, cooking, or playing music. Write as many activities as possible on your list and remember that you can always add to it over time. Commit yourself to doing at least one thing on your list every single day.

Remind yourself that when you do these activities, you are doing them because you deserve to be cared for. Tell yourself that you are doing these things because you love yourself. These activities are ways to be kind to yourself. If you put yourself down a lot, use self-care to start lifting yourself back up. This is a great way to improve your overall mood as well as building emotional strength and resilience. You will need to be in the best possible emotional condition in order to free yourself from social anxiety so there's no excuse to ignore your emotional needs at this time. Put yourself at the top of your list of priorities even if it feels strange at first. In a couple weeks' time you will start to notice that your feelings of self-worth and confidence have improved. You will notice a lift to your mood as well as your feelings of hopefulness and general enjoyment of life.

2 - Stop avoiding anxiety-inducing situations.

People with social anxiety often cancel plans with friends and may often fail to attend meetings and appointments. This is because the anxiety about the situation has become so big and so powerful that it's simply easier to give into it and avoid the situation entirely than it is to keep the appointment. Remember that it is possible to fool yourself into thinking you're canceling plans because you just don't feel like going out. But even when you're unaware of it, it's very possible that social anxiety is the true underlying cause behind all the events you intend on attending but never do. Avoidance also means leaving a situation as soon as anxiety appears, avoiding speaking to certain people who make you nervous or uncomfortable, and purposefully changing the way you do things in order to lessen the effect anxiety has on you. Hiding when you see someone walking towards you on the street or holding yourself back from trying new things also falls under the heading of avoidance.

The problem with avoidance is that it only serves to increase feelings of anxiety. Not attending an event or leaving when anxiety is at its peak means that you are telling yourself there is something you should genuinely fear and run away from. Every time you leave or avoid a situation entirely because anxiety has gotten the better of you, the anxiety gets stronger and you get weaker.

If you often cancel plans or fail to show up when you agree to be somewhere, you have to make a commitment to yourself to end this behavior. You have to tell yourself: No more canceling. Fear cannot hurt you. Avoidance can. Promise yourself to go where it is you're meant to be and stay there *at least* until your anxiety has reduced in severity or gone away completely. This is the only way to prove to yourself that you are stronger than the anxiety and that there is nothing to fear. Yes, you may have to endure some less-than-pleasant situations at the start. You will have to put yourself in spaces that you feel uncomfortable in. You will have to leave the house when you really don't want to. But doing so means proving to yourself that the fear you're experiencing is irrational. It means giving yourself a chance to practice using slow, rational thinking to defuse harmful racing thoughts. It means building resilience and strength against anxiety. This is the way to lasting recovery. Gradually exposing yourself to situations you would normally avoid will gradually reduce the amount of anxiety you experience when in them. You deserve to be able to live the life you want and actually enjoy being out in the world. This is the most promising way to pave that path for yourself.

3 - Tell someone how you're feeling.
Sometimes just saying how you're feeling out loud is enough to overcome anxiety in the moment. Imagine two people on a first date. They're probably both feeling nervous. If one of them is honest enough to say, *"I'm so nervous right now,"* the other

person is likely to admit the same feeling. Just getting that nervousness out in the open means that they can both laugh it off and create a bond while easing the magnitude of the worry they're each feeling in the moment. Relieving yourself of anxiety by sharing it with someone else can help in a few ways. Often just getting it off your chest is enough to calm things down for you. You can talk to someone you trust in a moment of intense anxiety or confide in a friend when things are calm. Both have long lasting benefits. Telling someone you trust might lead to a conversation about the anxiety and where it's coming from. It might help you unpack it, reason things out, and get perspective on your personal triggers. Telling someone you feel anxious often encourages others to share their own feelings of anxiety with you. This can make you feel a lot less alone in your current predicament. It helps to know that you're not the only person living with swells of social anxiety and you'd be surprised at just how many people share your sentiment when you're brave enough to start that conversation.

In the beginning of your journey, you might want to bring a friend with you when attending social events and this can be helpful as long as you don't use them as a long-term crutch. Having a friend who understands the feelings you struggle with means having an ally at your side. This could be a good person to help you remain in a situation until anxiety subsides. Before you go out together explain to your friend specifically how they can help you overcome social anxiety rather than having them act as a social life jacket ushering you around the room all night. Remember, they are not there to keep you *"safe"* as there is nothing truly to fear. Rather, they are there to assist you in your mission to face and overcome anxiety. Ask them to have you rate the level of anxiety you're feeling from 1-10 when you first arrive. Have them encourage you to remain in the situation until it drops below 5 or ideally below 3. Tell them ahead of time that maintaining eye contact with you can be very helpful during this process as it provides a safe focal point for you. Looking at your friend face-to-face like this can be calming, but it might also lead to giggle fits. All of this is positive. If you find yourself laughing genuinely, that's a good sign that your anxiety rating is starting to improve.

So, if there is someone in your life who you can trust to assist you through this process, by all means reach out and get them on board. If you don't have someone like this in your life, do not fear. You can tell just about anyone that you're feeling nervous in any given moment and still feel a little better for it. Basically, don't force yourself to suffer in silence. You'll be surprised at how many people tell you that they also struggle with social anxiety once you've placed your nervousness on the table.

Remember, *you are not alone and you do not have to fight this alone.* One word of caution worth mentioning here is that you should be careful not to open up to the wrong people. If there is someone in your life who is overly critical of you, or who is not willing to try to understand what you're going through, do not divulge your most sensitive issues to this person. Sharing information that is important to you is special and requires some level of trust and understanding. If you know someone is going to give you the brush off or mock you for what you're trying to achieve, keep them at arm's length. Not all relationships work at a deeper level, so if there are people in your life who you'd be safer keeping at surface level, by all means protect yourself by doing so. Not everyone deserves to know everything about you.

<u>4 - Use the "Shake It Off" technique.</u>
Anxiety is not something that only lives in the mind. It also has a number of bodily effects. Stiff and sore shoulders, neck, and back are common when dealing with tension. Upset stomachs and tiredness are common complaints. But most concerning are the effects of excess adrenaline. When experiencing fear or panic, our bodies produce adrenaline as part of the *"fight or flight"* response. This is an instinct that provides us with an increased heart rate and breathing rate so that we can be strong enough to fight off danger or run away from a major threat. The problem is that when we're experiencing anxiety, our bodies can misread the

situation and produce increased levels of adrenaline even when the fear we feel is irrational. If you've ever had a panic attack, you'll be familiar with becoming lightheaded, dizzy, or nauseas and experiencing tingling hands and feet, chest pains, and cold sweats as a result of excess adrenaline. These bodily sensations can actually make anxiety worse as they may be perceived as something more harmful like a heart attack or stroke.

Unfortunately, an anxious mind is more likely to perceive physical reactions to excess adrenaline as something more sinister. Because of this, you have to able to recognize that you are not having a heart attack and that you are not going to pass out. Rather, your body has created too much adrenaline for the situation at hand. Getting rid of excess adrenaline isn't easy but it is possible and helpful in calming yourself down.

There are a number of non-human animals who use *"shaking"* as a way of ridding themselves of negative sensations. Yes, dogs, jungle cats, and bears shake their bodies from side to side when drying off after a swim, but they also do so after experiencing fear, danger, or a fight. This is, in essence, a way of physically ridding themselves of the tension the situation has caused them to feel. It's a way for them to push the *"reset"* button, so to speak. Humans do not have an equivalent to shaking, yet anxiety, fear, and tension are typically felt physically as well as emotionally. For this reason, finding a way to physically *"shake it off"* can be very effective when it comes to eliminating excess adrenaline and calming down.

If you recognize yourself becoming anxious, do something about it. Go outside for a run. Do some jumping jacks. Turn on some music and dance it out. Go swimming. Do whatever you can to physically work the anxiety out of your body. In addition to reducing feelings of anxiety, exercise can cause heightened levels of serotonin and endorphins, or *"feel good"* chemicals. Don't underestimate the power that exercise can hold over anxiety. The next time you feel anxiety rising, don't sit around the house overthinking things. Instead, get out and start moving. Push your own physical reset button. Rid yourself of the physical tension attached to anxiety. Afterwards you will find it easier to process the thoughts beneath those feelings.

5 - Practice breathing exercises.
Breathing exercises are beneficial for a few reasons. They can be a great way to steady your mind before, during, and after a surge of anxiety. They can also help reduce the amount of oxygen you're taking in during a panic attack. Remember that panic attacks usually send your body into fight or flight mode. This means unconsciously taking faster, shallow breaths so as to take in more oxygen for the benefit of pumping up your muscles for a potential fight. When high levels of oxygen exist without the presence of a true threat, the result is light-headedness, dizziness, tingling shaky hands, loss of feeling in the face or lips, and general feelings of potentially passing out. All of these feelings can lead to increased panic. Use breathing exercises can help spare you from being overwhelmed by the effects of taking in too much oxygen.

There are three ways you might approach measured breathing. All of these focus on consciously exhaling for longer than you inhale so that you can even out your oxygen levels and prevent hyperventilation. The first way of doing this is simply counting 5's and 7's as you breathe. Breathe in for 5 counts, and out for 7. When you do this, and any other breathing exercise, place a hand on your tummy. Rather than feeling your shoulders rising and falling, you should feel your stomach extending outward with each inhale, and inward with each exhale. Being mindful of this will prevent hyperventilation and head rushes. The second way is to breathe naturally but to focus on exhaling for as long as you possibly can. After each inhale, blow out as much air as you can squeeze out of your lungs. Tighten up your lips so that the air escapes you slowly rather than huffing it out all at once.

Remember to keep that hand on your tummy so you know you're breathing from your diaphragm, not high up in your chest. The third thing you might want to try is doing some visualization while you breathe. As you inhale, picture yourself taking in positive energy in the form of a white light. Imagine this white light filling you with serenity, peace, and contentment. As you exhale, picture yourself blowing out black smoke. This is all the negative energy escaping your body; all your fear and sadness, all the things holding you down, and of course, anxiety itself. Repeat this exercise, making sure each exhale is longer than each inhale, until you feel yourself relax. Whichever breathing technique works best for you, just remember to always focus on the exhale. Breathing exercises like these are good to get used to doing on a daily basis for maintaining a regular sense of daily calm, but they can also be used in a moment of intense anxiety.

Just remember that when you use breathing exercises while in a heightened state, it can take around 10-15 minutes until you feel like you have fully recovered. This amount of time will gradually lessen as you get used to defusing anxiety in this way.

6 - Choose where and when you socialize.

Remember that anxiety often centers around circumstances we cannot control. So in order to gain some control when you're first attempting to beat anxiety, do things on your own terms. Don't use this as a way of avoiding anxiety-inducing situations. This is not a hard and fast rule for the future, nor is it an excuse to only go places you feel comfortable or safe. This is just something to use in the beginning to build resilience and prove to yourself that you're strong enough to endure social situations. Make sure you're setting yourself up for success. Try socializing in places you like spending time or at events that you know won't be terribly uncomfortable. Go with people you feel safe with. Attend social situations that you are likely to enjoy and think of positively. If you've been avoiding social situations for some time, this is going to be a very important way of getting yourself back out there. You do not have to begin by throwing yourself into your most dreaded scenario.

Be gentle with yourself when facing fears or you'll risk doing more harm than good. There is no use in attending events you will genuinely dislike just for the sake of trying to dismantle anxiety. If a quiet place with a small crowd is more appealing to you than a giant outdoor festival, choose the smaller venue in the early days. Socialize at small get togethers in friends' homes rather than noisy bars if that's more enticing. Choose to meet friends for daytime coffee rather than nighttime drinks if that seems more comfortable. Being in control of where, when, and with whom you socialize is smart when you're still learning how to slow down your thoughts. You can (and should) always build from there. When you feel comfortable with one situation, take a step up the next time you go out. Give yourself a little bit more of a challenge each time you successfully face a social situation. Be in control of your progress. Don't throw yourself into the deep end and don't hold yourself back when you've outgrown the shallow end.

7 - <u>Try to have some fun.</u>

Social events are not intended to be torturous. Remember that. Most social events are designed to be fun, helpful, or informative. Humans have a fundamental need for socialization. We are meant to live and function in groups. Being around other people is good for you. It should offer a space where you can get out of your head, not retreat into it. So try, when you're out, to have a good time. Try to focus on enjoying yourself rather than giving all your energy to anxiety.

Tell the anxiety to take a hike for a minute while you catch up with a friend you haven't seen in a long time. If a song that you love comes on, let yourself listen to it, sing along, or dance. If you have a great outfit that you haven't been able to wear out yet because anxiety has been holding you hostage, go out and show it off. Is there a restaurant you love that you haven't felt able to go to in a while? Grab a friend and go eat your favorite dish. Focus on harvesting the positive feelings that exist in the social world whenever possible. Where you place your focus is up to you. You

have to try to recognize when your mind is focusing on the
negative possibilities, or the scary stuff, or the "what-ifs" and tell
it to stop. Regain your focus. Place it on the enjoyable stuff. Place
it on the people that warm your heart. Place it on the things that
make you feel good about the world. Practice this again and
again.

Attend social situations that you know you will enjoy, even if just
a little bit. This is a powerful way to start changing the way you
think and feel about socializing. It's a way to replace the negative
associations you have with socializing with new positive ones.
You will gain control over your thoughts the more you try to.
Anyone can train themselves to think differently. No one is a lost
cause. Give yourself a chance to feel good when you're out.
That's what life is about.

The Power of Change - Lesson 3

Take a moment now to write a self care promise to yourself. In
addition to compiling a list of activities you enjoy, make a
commitment to engage in enjoyable daily activities for the sole
purpose of feeling good.

What have you been withholding from yourself lately?
What do you rarely make time to do anymore?
Is there time in your days that you're currently wasting that could
be better used as self care time?
Make a decision to treat yourself more kindly and dedicate
yourself to doing so.
Choose something from your list every day and do whatever you
can to treat yourself with love and kindness.

Everyday Practices to Combat Anxiety Fast

So far, we've covered a few ways to deal with social anxiety before, during, and after emotionally activating situations. You know that you have to face your social fears, remain in situations until you feel yourself calming down, and reflect on your progress regularly. You've read a few tips on long-term coping techniques including talking to a friend, gaining some control over social situations, and most importantly committing yourself to a daily self-care routine. Self-care is a powerful way to build self-esteem, maintain longer periods of good mood and general relaxation, build resilience and strength, and also manage the toll life takes on you. But there are still quite a number of things you can do on a daily basis that will make you far less shakable in the hands of anxiety.

It is important to take daily measures against social anxiety rather than waiting for it to strike. Prevention of anxiety is a powerful tool to have on your side. After all, why wait for social anxiety to launch an attack before taking action? If you know it's always just around the corner, there are things you can do to keep it in its place.

Think of your mood like a set of traffic lights. When your mind is on green, things are going well. You feel fairly settled and calm. You're happy or at least content. You're sleeping well and things are going pretty smoothly. You're particularly resilient when things go wrong and find that you can recover with relative ease. When your mood is on amber, your mind is starting to feel a bit rattled. It won't take much to tip you over the edge, but things could go either way. You're feeling a little unsettled but still relatively solid. If things go wrong you might be strong enough to handle it, but you could get thrown off your game. On red, your mind is in crisis mode. Anxiety may have a strong hold on you.

You may enter a period of low mood or feel like you have no control. You may feel very unstable and alone. It may be hard to see the good things amidst all the negativity you're feeling and it would be difficult to bring yourself back to green or amber if something went wrong.

The aim in preventative techniques is to actively treat the mind when it's in green or amber territory. This way, it never gets a chance to go to red. This is why I suggest *daily* self-care rather than using self-care to defuse difficult emotions in a crisis. The more kindness you offer yourself when you are on green or amber, the less likely you will be to ever get to red. With good self-care, times on green will last longer, and times on amber will be more likely to bounce back to green rather than increasing to red. Keep this in mind as you read through this section. Remember that preventing anxiety from ever striking is more powerful than any coping mechanism you can use in heightened times. This is because preventative measures happen when you're at your strongest, most capable, and most hopeful.

Use times when you're feeling good to advance even further in your personal development. Don't use them to be complacent or to wait for things to spontaneously go wrong. Think of it like physical exercise. If you haven't done any physical exercise in a long time, you're really going to feel it the first day back at the gym. You'll be out of breath and your muscles will hurt for days. But if you attend the gym a few times a week, maintaining physical fitness is easier and it actually starts to feel good. The things that were hard in the beginning will be little more than a warm-up. The same goes for your emotional wellbeing. If you work on feelings of confidence, good mood, self-approval and self-worth when you're already feeling strong, those emotional muscles are going to be in great shape when you really need them. If you feel yourself moving into amber, recognize it and push yourself back to green by increasing your self-care, taking special care of your physical self, and getting plenty of rest. You get the gist. Now have a look at the following list of ways you can keep your mind in the green and get the most out of your self-progression.

7 Realistic Methods to Feel Better and More Confident

1 - Limit your screen time.

It's important to be honest with yourself when evaluating the effect screen time is having on you. Most of us have a serious attachment to our mobile phones, tablets, and computers. We spend our days checking texts, emails, DMs, news feeds, and social media accounts with reckless abandon. We no longer allow ourselves to leave our phone at home, even when we're only going to be out for a matter of minutes. We are constantly contactable and constantly stimulated. This creates a very high pressure way of life that has very much become the social norm. But this way of life is hard on the human psyche. Feeling like we have to respond to every message we get throughout the day means we're living life without boundaries. We allow people to contact us regardless of the time of day or what we're experiencing as individuals in any given moment. Two decades ago, it would've been unthinkable to live our lives this way.

Furthermore, as a society we have become addicted to this way of life and profoundly impatient as a result of it. Think about it. What do we do when we're waiting? We stare at our phones. We could be waiting for a friend to arrive, waiting for the bus, waiting for an appointment, waiting for anything at all and you can bet we'll be staring down and scrolling. We have lost the ability to self-soothe via any means outside of screen time. We have lost the ability to simply sit and be quiet. Screens are the first and last things we look at each day. We feel lost without them. This is something that has to be addressed. Because the less we know how to soothe ourselves without screens, and the more over-stimulated and impatient we become, the higher our anxiety levels will rise.

The fact is, we've stopped giving ourselves a chance to hear our own thoughts. We rarely take time to actively listen to ourselves and just feel our emotions. Rather, when ill feelings surface, we distract ourselves. We shut it down. This is problematic when trying to address something like anxiety or depression. We have to give ourselves time and space to listen to our inner selves. We need to literally switch off our devices and give our eyes and brains a break. We need to take time every day to stop seeking distraction and cut the ties between ourselves and our phones. We have to go for a walk and leave the phone behind. We have to cut through the binge watching and do something creative instead. We have to stop putting pressure on ourselves to respond to messages right away, and give ourselves the freedom to reply in our own time. We have to take some of the urgency out of our relationships with other people.

So at this time, I suggest that you think about how screen time is affecting you and set some rules for yourself. If you're wasting time online rather than doing something nice for yourself, make a resolve to replace some of that screen time with self-care. If you let friends and family contact you at all hours, free yourself from this pressure by imposing a cut-off time for replies each evening. Make a resolve not to be distracted by personal texts at work, or work texts at home. If you feel like you're constantly over-stimulated, start by giving yourself 2 or 3 screen-free hours every day and work up from there.

Chances are, the less screen time you have, the less anxious you will feel. You'll start wanting more and more screen-free time because you'll realize that there is an intense feeling of freedom and relaxation when you finally tackle screen overuse. The aim here is to slow things down and start listening to yourself rather than seeking distraction and ignoring your inner thoughts and feelings. This could be a little bit jarring if you've been using screen time as a way of avoiding your own difficult thoughts and feelings, but doing so means giving yourself a chance to finally face those things and start to heal. If you reduce the amount of external stimulation you're subjected to, you are more likely to feel calmer in general and more in control of your life. This means having a much more solid foundation from which to approach the anxiety you are currently experiencing. It's too hard to try to rid yourself of anxiety if your mind is always in a heightened state. Giving yourself plenty of time away from screens and unnecessary intellectual stimulation means reserving some energy for yourself. This way you'll have the freedom to slow things down and secure some much needed quiet time for yourself.

2 - Take care of yourself physically.

It should come as no great surprise that taking good care of our physical selves is extremely important to our emotional wellbeing. Poor physical health can lead to poor mental health and vice versa. The mind-body connection is indisputable. When we neglect our physical health, we are telling ourselves that we are not worthy of proper care. Eating the wrong foods, avoiding fresh air and exercise, and withholding sleep from ourselves or refusing to get out of bed will not have a positive impact on how we feel emotionally. The fact is, being unable to get control of your physical life could mean being unable to control your emotional life, and in any period of personal development, having control over our lives is key. We have to get real with ourselves and show ourselves that we are worthy of the good stuff in life. This means committing ourselves to eating right, getting plenty of time outdoors, exercising regularly, and getting into healthy sleep routines.

Now I am not suggesting that you go from zero to hero overnight. If you really don't like the gym, I'm not going to suggest that you join one. Rather, I am suggesting that you think about how well you are caring for yourself honestly and realistically. Seek out anything you might be able to do better. If your eating or drinking habits are out of control, consider setting some rules and parameters for yourself. This is a good way of gaining a sense of self-discipline while valuing your own health. If you spend too much time indoors with the curtains closed, start opening the windows and getting out for more walks. Remember that exercise is great for working out excess nervous energy as well as helping you sleep better at night. Being around nature can also have immensely positive effects on your mood and general outlook on life, so encourage yourself to take walks at local beaches, parks, or forest trails, or visit scenic places nearby when you have time. Keep a close eye on your alcohol and caffeine intake as they can both cause increases in anxiety and panic. Be as good to your body as you can. This method of self-care can only have positive effects on your life.

So too, if you are struggling with pain or fatigue, you may start to notice an improvement when caring for yourself better. Losing weight can have a dramatic impact on generalized pains and fatigue, as can eating right and taking in plenty of nutrients. All in all, try to do what you can to limit abuse to your body. You deserve to be cared for physically, emotionally, and intellectually.

3 - Get rid of insomnia.

Insomnia is a common complaint for people experiencing anxiety of any sort. It may be something that comes and goes or something you've lived with for a long time. For most people, insomnia worsens during periods of personal conflict, difficult emotions, daunting upcoming events, loss of control over one's life, and periods of waiting. These are all situations that can cause anxiety to increase as well, and where anxiety lives, racing or obsessive thoughts may also become imbedded. Dealing with conflict can be extremely disruptive to one's life. Waiting to find out about a new job, waiting for test results about a physical illness, or generally feeling like your life is in limbo can be distressing and may lead to sleeplessness.

For social anxiety sufferers, an upcoming social event or work meeting can be very hard to stop thinking about. Obsessive and cyclical thoughts are common when something like this is looming in the future. And of course, it's not exactly easy to sleep when your mind won't stop going, so learning to beat insomnia is a good skill to have on your side. After all, tomorrow's work meeting isn't going to be any less daunting if you've had a terrible night's sleep.

There are a few things you can do to get your mind to settle down and drift off to sleep, and it's worth trying until you find something that works for you. Some methods focus on your physical body while others work directly on the mind. Physically, you can make sure you're getting plenty of exercise and fresh air during the daytime. Spend plenty of time in sunlight as this helps restore your body's natural rhythms. Avoid sleeping in late in the morning so that your body is actually tired come nightfall. Avoid caffeinated beverages after noon; even if you think it's not affecting you, it probably is. Try drinking some valerian tea before bed. Place some lavender oil on your temples or on a tissue near your pillow. Use an eye mask or ear plugs if necessary to create a more sleep friendly environment. Make sure your sheets and pillows are inviting. They should be clean, comfortable, and the right temperature. Try to get to bed around the same time every evening so that your body clock is working for you, not against you. Turn off any screens about an hour before you intend to sleep. Having the TV on while you sleep could be encouraging you to think rather than to relax. Choose a book, meditation, beauty treatment, or hygiene ritual to unwind instead.

For your mind, focus on relieving yourself of obsessive thoughts. If there is something you can't stop thinking about, write it down. This should not be used as a way to think more heavily about it or to get yourself more worked up. Rather, you should use this as a means of releasing yourself from these thoughts. Write down your worries and tell yourself to let them go for the night. Recognize when you've done all you can about something and tell yourself to let it go. Recognize when something is out of your hands and let it go. Use meditation and visualization to rid yourself of unhelpful thoughts. Visualize your worries drifting away from you.

Remember, holding them too close is only harming you. If there is nothing you can do about something, obsessing over it isn't going to help. Meditate to bring your focus back to calm territory. Focus on the feeling of breath on your upper lip as you exhale. Focusing on just one physical sensation will help other thoughts to drift away. Any time you feel your focus slipping, pull it back. Feel that breath on your upper lip. Focus on that sensation alone. Practicing meditation and gaining control of your mind like this will be valuable in your waking life as well as helping you sleep at night. Being able to silence racing thoughts is a wonderful skill to have on your side. You don't have to sit in any special position or breathe in any special way if you don't want to. Just lay on your bed and focus on one single part of your being. Counting techniques can be helpful for insomnia too. Although things like this are not helpful for controlling anxiety long term, they can be very helpful when it comes to drifting off to sleep. So go ahead and count down backwards from 100 in 3's. Or name boys' names from A-Z. Test yourself on capital cities starting with M. Meaningless exercises like this can be helpful to cut through busy nighttime brains. They are not stimulating enough to keep you awake so if your brain insists on thinking, give it something to think about that's boring and inconsequential. Eventually it'll give up the ghost and let you get some shut-eye.

4 - Get organized.
Remember that things like chaos and unpredictability are particularly hard on the mind. Being organized and prepared for upcoming events can help you feel like you have a better hold on your life. Organization is the antidote to chaos, so think about some ways you can limit the amount of unpredictability in your life in favor of control. Morning and evening rituals can be a great way to grab hold of the reins if life is overwhelming you. Things like diary keeping, list writing, and scheduling can help reduce

the impact the unpredictable stuff has on you. Keeping to a strict routine in the first few hours of the day can also be helpful. You may wish you start the day with meditation or exercise. You might like to get all your housework done in the morning or implement an indulgent breakfast ritual. You might like to start your day by writing a to-do list and thinking about how you're going to attack the day.

Similarly, having a reliable bedtime routine can help you sleep better at night. Doing the same things at the same time each night creates structure, and there are few things the human mind likes more than structure and reliability! The aim here is to reduce the amount of unknowns in the course of your days. Anxiety is rooted in fear and social anxiety in particular relates strongly to that which we cannot predict. You can actively combat this by creating more things that you *can* predict. More things you can *control*. There are a lot of ways to harvest this type of predictability. Meal plans and exercise routines can be helpful. Keeping your home organized can have a significant impact on stress and anxiety. Getting your papers in order so that you know where everything is means being in control of your surroundings. You get the gist.

If you feel like your life is lacking organization or control, think about some ways of harvesting that for yourself. Address the things that are particularly bothersome in your life or try writing a new routine for yourself. Just remember to be realistic with any goals. It's not easy to change everything in your life all at once, so start small. You can always work up from there.

5 - Consider meditation and visualization.
There are many forms of meditation so before deciding this isn't for you, consider these three things: Meditation does not always occur when you are sitting crosslegged and profoundly connected to the world around you. Meditation is not something that people are either good at or bad at. And meditation takes practice. Most people who have tried meditation have thought that they're *"not*

good at it" at the start. This is because meditation is a practice of gaining control of one's thoughts and feelings. It isn't easy and it rarely comes naturally. It is something that requires practice and determination. It's important to accept that the mind will always do what it can to wander off in different directions and this is okay. When attempting to get to a meditative state, the trick is to not get frustrated by this wandering.

Rather, when your mind wanders away from your chosen focus, simply allow yourself to listen to your thoughts and then gently pull your focus back. The more often you do this, the better you will get at it. You will soon find that remaining focussed becomes easier and that your mind will wander less and less often. Learning to control your thoughts like this can have immeasurable benefits on anxiety. If you get good at it, you can bring meditative thinking into emotionally activating situations. You can actively silence anxious thoughts and block out excess *"noise"* coming from negative thought processes. This can have profound benefits to you in social situations that would normally cause you to feel a rise in anxiety.

If you want to become involved with meditation or visualization there are a few ways you might get started. Taking a guided meditation class is usually a good place to start as it can provide structure you might not otherwise be exposed to. If you are a beginner, I'd advise you to find a class that lasts around 30 minutes rather than trying to last longer than that. This way you won't be overwhelmed or disheartened if you have a hard time maintaining focus for the entire class. You may wish to start at home with a relaxation track online or a video on YouTube. Or you may just want to sit or lay down quietly in a comfortable position and practice your own method. There is no right or wrong way to practice meditation.

Before you begin, try to set an intension for yourself. Think about what you would like to get out of your meditation. You may like to visualize the way you'd like to be in social settings. Picture yourself being perceived the way you'd like to be. Picture yourself handling social situations the way you'd like to. Picture yourself confident and self-assured in situations you'd normally experience as anxiety-inducing and daunting. As you hone your meditation and visualization skills, start bringing them out into real life with you. When you feel anxiety swelling inside you, tap into that quiet place inside. Feel the anxiety and let it pass like you would with any other unwelcome thought.

6 - Take care of your self-image.

Many times social anxiety and self-esteem are closely linked. Periods of social anxiety often creep up when we're not happy with the way we think others are perceiving us. We might not like the way we look or we might not feel proud of the way our home or belongings look. And similarly, the more social anxiety we feel, the less likely we are to feel good about ourselves. In times when social anxiety is at its peak, we are less likely to address the things we don't like about ourselves. We might neglect to get a decent haircut or update our wardrobe because our sense of self-worth is low. But the fact is, the better we feel about ourselves on the outside, the more likely we are to feel confident in social situations.

Neglecting to take care of our appearance could be an excuse to continue feeding into social anxiety. It's also a good way to neglect showing ourselves love and care. The important thing is to make sure you're not trying to look good for other people. The point is to look good for yourself so that you actually want to get out and about. There's nothing worse than avoiding socializing because you hate your current appearance. So if you have been neglecting the way you look or dress, treat yourself to a makeover. Don't wait until you lose weight to buy yourself some nice clothes. Treat yourself. Get a new hairdo or treat yourself to an extravagant beauty treatment. Get a professional massage or take a spa day. Treating yourself this way can help your self-esteem and benefit your feelings of self-worth. You may find that you're walking with your head up again just because you feel better about your self-image. You deserve to feel proud of how you look.

In addition to taking care of your appearance, putting the same amount of care into your living space can also have a significant impact on your self-esteem. If your house or bedroom is in dire need of a makeover, make it happen. Get some new furniture or paint your walls. Get rid of clutter and move things around for a sense of change. Give yourself a fresh outlook on your living space by physically changing the way you exist in it. Turn chairs so that they're facing new directions. Take advantage of areas that benefit from good natural light. Invest in some new sheets and cushions. Everyone needs a moment to freshen things up occasionally, especially when embarking on a period of self-progression. So think about what sort of visual stimulation surrounds you when you're at home.

Does your living space make you feel good about yourself? Or has it become drab and stifling? Are there any projects you once started but never finished? If so, now is the time to get them done. Does your living space resemble who you want to be or who you once were? Are you surrounded by stuff your ex left in the house when you broke up? If so, get rid of it. If there are things you don't like about your living space, do something about it now. You will be surprised at just how much of an impact it can have on your mood and sense of self.

7 - Take time to just be.
In addition to limiting screen time and trying out meditation, try to take some time each day to just sit quietly and switch off. This is something that people rarely do anymore for a variety of reasons. Our lives are busy, we have too much to do. We're not used to existing without stimulation so doing so can actually be uncomfortable at first. But this is a bad sign because it means we're not taking enough time to listen to our thoughts. We're losing the ability to sit quietly and do nothing. In order to reduce the intellectual energy we're using up each day, it's important to

give our minds a break. Remember, anxiety is taxing and tiring for the mind.

So consider using your lunch break for lunch, instead of using it to run errands or write emails. Think about using the first hour after work to relax, instead of using it to run around cleaning the house, cooking, or getting prepared for the following day. Resolve yourself to actively reserve some time each day to just be quiet. Consider doing this for yourself. Sit somewhere comfortable where you are unlikely to be disturbed. This can be in your home, in your car, or in a nice scenic location. Whatever works for you.

Remove all stimulation for 15-30 minutes. Turn off screens, podcasts, and radios. Don't read or peruse magazines. Put your schedule and your to-do list away. Remove all distraction and just let yourself just be. Exist in the space around you, stripped of stimulation and pressure. Released of responsibilities and constraints. Just you and your thoughts. Your physical body, quiet and relieved. This is a gift you can give to yourself. A way to remember who you are and what you want out of life. A time to reflect on your strengths. A break, a *real* break, from all the things you have to do each day. Being able to exist in silence is a sign of a very healthy mind.

The Power of Change - Lesson 4

Think about how well you look after yourself the way things are right now.

Are there things that you are particularly good at?
What strengths do you have when it comes to taking care of yourself?

Remember that it's important to hold onto your strengths, to celebrate them and use them to spur you on to do even more. Are you doing anything to combat your anxiety on a daily basis? Are you taking good care of yourself?

If not, why? Is it because you don't value yourself enough? Do you feel powerless? Are you afraid of failing?

Do you consider yourself unworthy of care and concern? Are you stuck in a rut? Are your energy levels too low to take proper care of yourself?

Reread the daily activities above and dedicate yourself to doing at least 5 of them every single day. Keep track of what you're doing for yourself in a journal or on your phone and be dedicated to offering yourself more. I promise you that after just one week of caring for yourself like this you will notice a change in your mood, your self-esteem, and your anxiety levels. You will begin to view yourself as stronger in the face of social anxiety and more capable of reaching your personal goals.

Part Two: Real Change Now

Dealing With Emotionally Activating Situations

Now that you are armed with knowledge and you're taking good care of yourself both physically and mentally, you should feel ready to start putting your knowledge into practice. It's okay if you're still feeling some trepidation at the thought of socializing. These things take time to adjust to so make sure you don't put too much pressure on yourself. You might need to take some baby steps in order to reach your goal. Try to be kind to yourself during this process. Self-progression is a sign of strength and determination. Remember that in facing and trying to change the limitations you live with, you are showing an immense amount of courage. This is nothing to scoff at! Always bare in mind that positive change doesn't always move in one direction. You may take two steps forward and one step back at times. You might feel better one day and worse the next. This is normal. It isn't something to beat yourself up about and it isn't a reason to give up on yourself. If you're having a rough day or a social experience doesn't go the way you hoped it would, treat yourself with extra care and encourage yourself to get back up and try again the next day.

In life, all of us will be exposed to a variety of social situations, each with their own intricacies. Some will be easy, natural, and emotionally uneventful. Others will not. Everyone faces social situations that are especially challenging, and for those of us experiencing social anxiety, these will be the hardest ones to endure. For instance, on a good day, running into someone you have a positive relationship with while walking down the street is unlikely to cause a rise in your anxiety. Conversely, running into someone you're in a conflict with on a day when you're already not feeling great about yourself could feel like your thoughts are fracturing into a million pieces, your head is spinning, and you want nothing more than to run and hide. This section is going to address how to cope with some specific emotionally activating situations such as chance run-ins, dealing with conflict, and feeling as though you are on display, as well as preparing for the unexpected.

One of the hardest things to cope with in the social sphere is the fear of running into someone unexpectedly. This is something that most people experience at one time or another, regardless of if they experience social anxiety or not. The fact is, relationships play a significant role in human existence. We are not alone on this earth. We have friends, family, significant others, bosses, colleagues and acquaintances to name a few. And by the same rite, we also have ex-friends, family members with whom we are estranged, ex-partners and ex-lovers, bosses who hated or fired us, colleagues we never got along with, and acquaintances we wish we could walk by without acknowledging because we have virtually nothing to talk to them about. Relationships are complicated and they exist on a very wide spectrum. The thing is, we can't avoid other people all the time. They are a part of the world we live in. What we can do is become stronger and happier in ourselves. With practice, we can learn to focus on putting our energy into feeding the positive relationships in our lives and just shrug off the negative ones, rather than letting them hurt or upset us.

There are a lot of places you could potentially run into someone you don't want to see, especially if you live in the same town or tend to frequent the same places. Walking down the street, riding the bus, grabbing a coffee, grocery shopping, you name it. Avoidance is not going to serve you when it comes to chance run-ins. If you try to avoid running into someone by going to different stores or taking different routes to work, etc., you are giving that person, and the anxiety, power and control over you while allowing fear to dominate your life. No one should be given the power to dictate where you can and cannot go comfortably.

Freedom is a fundamental human need. We have to feel free to live our lives and do the things we want to do in order to maintain the quality of life we deserve. So how can you exist comfortably in the world without fear of being subjected to a conversation you're not prepared for?

First off, you can take some time to think about what it is you're actually afraid of.

Are you afraid of being put on the spot? Of having to come up with something to say?

Are you afraid that you'll be so blindsided by the sight of someone that you won't be able to be your best self? That you'll appear flustered and uncomfortable? That you'll stutter or say something stupid? That you'll just freeze up?

Do you dread awkward encounters in general?

Is your self-esteem poor right now?

Do you wish you looked differently or had better things going on in your life?

Is there someone causing you pain right now that you just can't bare to see?

Take a few minutes to think about this. If there is someone or a number of people you wouldn't like to run into unexpectedly, start by identifying who those people are. If this is something you're really struggling with, it may help to think on it for a few days. The mind isn't always ready to unpack all its thoughts and feelings on the spot, so if you're drawing a blank, it might be a bit easier and more natural for you to simply keep that conversation alive in your mind and let these thoughts come to you over a period of time.

You might be more likely to think of something relevant while you're driving, showering, or folding laundry than you would be if you were holding a pencil and staring at a blank page. There is not right or wrong way to attack these things so just do what works for you. It may be beneficial to write down the names of individuals whose presence you find emotionally activating and slowly unpack what it is about potential encounters with them that's filling you with dread. Similarly, if you have a hard time narrowing down who it is exactly that you're afraid of running into, or you think you're just scared of running into anyone at all, try coming up with a list of people you *wouldn't* mind running into instead and think about what it is about their presence that *doesn't* fill you with dread. Feelings of all or nothing can be hard to see through, so this might help if the mere idea of running into another human being is just too overwhelming right now.

The aim is to think more clearly about the specific fears you're experiencing and the feelings attached to them. Go easy on yourself during this process, and as always, do not use this exercise to feel bad about yourself. Remember that this is all very common. It is not a sign that something is terribly wrong with you. If you find that thoughts of someone in particular are upsetting you, take a break. Don't force yourself to do something that's only making you feel worse. The aim here is to simply connect with the feelings you associate with certain individuals. Once you connect with those feelings, you can identify what specific fears are attached to them.

For instance, you may dread running into your ex for a variety of reasons. You may still have feelings for them, you may still feel hurt by them, you may be afraid of seeing them with a new lover, you may feel ashamed or embarrassed about something you did while in that relationship, you may feel under confident because you haven't quite bounced back yet since your break-up. There are a million and one thoughts and feelings you could have attached to your ex, and if you're likely to run into them at one time or another, it's no wonder you feel nervous about seeing them unexpectedly. It's only natural. But if you can identify the specific fears and feelings you have in regards to that person, you can start to challenge them and turn them around. You can start by thinking about how they'd feel if they saw you unexpectedly. Isn't it likely that they'd also be taken off guard? That they might feel uncomfortable, nervous, or awkward? Isn't it possible that they may share some of the same feelings you have? That they might be experiencing guilt or sadness? Even if they seem like the most cool, calm, and collected person on earth, isn't it possible that they would be as unprepared and shaken as you would be if you had a chance meeting? It would be helpful to remember that the feelings you are experiencing are not a sign that something is wrong with you. Chance meetings with exes are something most people dread, not just those who are *"weak"* or *"broken"*. It is only natural to feel a bit gross when you see someone you're not ready to see.

Using the same example, what else might you do to prepare for an accidental run-in? You might want to briefly practice a conversation in your mind. Think to yourself, *"If I saw this person and had to talk to them, the things I'd like to say are…"*.

For instance, you might think about which subjects are safe to bring up and which are not. It might be wise to steer clear of any questions that are too personal or any that are about dating new people as these could be emotionally activating and disrespectful of both your personal boundaries. You might simply aim to be polite as though you were merely talking to an acquaintance and stick to questions about work and family. Plan to talk about something you've recently accomplished or something you're proud of right now to help you feel empowered instead of giving in to feelings of inferiority or discomfort.
Holding onto things you feel good about is as much about maintaining self-confidence as it is about appearing to be at your best. You might also plan to keep an unexpected conversation brief by planning how to exit it gracefully.

Saying something like, *"Well I've got to get to work, but it was nice to see you"* could mean getting out of the conversation before any awkwardness strikes. Think ahead about if you will hug this person when you see them or if you'll maintain your physical distance. Think about if you'd rather just wave or nod hello instead of getting into a conversation with them at all. If it would be safer for you emotionally to leave it at that, then plan to handle it that way rather than being strong-armed into having a conversation you don't want to have. Having a plan intact can reduce anxiety because you will not only feel prepared when you see that person, but you will also feel in control of the situation.

Finally, within the same example, in order to prepare for an accidental run-in with this person, use visualization and positive self-talk to build up your inner strength. Picture yourself talking to this person and being completely unfazed by their presence. Picture yourself coming across exactly the way you'd like to. Picture yourself walking tall and keeping your head up. Imagine yourself feeling strong and unbothered. Imagine feeling confident. Remind yourself that you are still standing. You may have endured a situation with this person that was painful but you are carrying on. You're still living your life. This person does not have power over you. This person is not allowed to dictate how you feel about yourself. You are in control of yourself and your life. You do not need to carry negative emotions about this person with you forever. You are free to be you regardless of how your relationships have affected you.

This type of thinking and planning can be beneficial when you're worried about running into anyone you'd rather not see. It's not just for exes. Remember that a lot of times, the people we don't want to see are equally nervous about seeing us. Even when they seem like they're not bothered, they could hiding the same type of feelings you are experiencing. There are two things that are important to remember.

1 - That you allow yourself time to think, plan, and prepare for possible run-ins without obsessing over them. Overthinking can be dangerous and may serve to increase anxiety in the long run. So set yourself some parameters and limits. Once you have unpacked your feelings and devised a plan, tell yourself that that's enough. You are strong and you are ready. Nitpicking about every possible subject that may arise and dwelling on your negative emotions could be counterintuitive. It's okay to think and feel, but try to protect yourself from wallowing. If thoughts of someone are upsetting you greatly, give it some time before you fully unpack it. Sometimes our wounds need to heal before we can fully move past something.

2 - If you run into someone you didn't want to see, let go of the encounter once it has passed. It can be tempting to indulge in reruns of the conversation in your head. You may find yourself thinking about what you should've said or what you could've said better. You may feel embarrassed or unsure about how you came across to that person. You may be overly concerned with how you looked in that moment. But giving in to obsessive thoughts or unhelpful reruns like this is rarely a good idea. You will never be able to change that conversation.

Therefore, dwelling on it is a waste of your time. Remind yourself that the person you ran into is more likely to be thinking about how they came across. They may be obsessing about the things they said instead of even remembering what you said. That is simply how the human mind works. So try to let go of awkward encounters when they happen. Don't give them too much of your energy. They are almost always harmless and really are just a mediocre part of human life. They have no baring on your life on a grander scale.

The second emotionally activating situation worth discussing is dealing with conflict. Again, this is something that all humans face time and time again, but for people living with social anxiety, conflict can be completely disarming. If you have a hard time carrying on a conversation with someone at the best of times, talking to them in the worst of times isn't going to be easy. Conflict is uncomfortable. It can make you feel like you're in the wrong, even when you aren't. It can be painful, especially when you're conflicting with someone you care about. It can make you feel bad about yourself, rejected, guilty or ashamed. And of course, it can make you feel anxious.

There are endless reasons that conflicts arise. It could be about something that happened at work, with your family, or amongst friends. You may be going through a break-up, facing disciplinary action at work, you may have been betrayed or let down, perhaps a conversational misunderstanding led to a fight with someone you care about. You might be being bullied at work or in another similar environment. Having to walk into volatile atmospheres can be extremely disruptive to your life as well as having devastating effects on your mood and self-esteem. Add social anxiety to the mix and a conflict can begin to take over your life.

In order to minimize the effect conflict has on you, take these four steps. First, get perspective. When a conflict starts to get the better of you, you have to shrink it down in your mind. Look at the bigger picture. Widen your view of the situation. Instead of thinking about how this thing is making you feel now, think about how important it really is in the grand scheme of things.

Is this something that is going to be important in another month? How about in a year or two?
Is the person you are in a conflict with worth the amount of energy you're giving them?
Yes, you may feel hurt, but does their opinion of you really matter in the long run?
Should they be allowed to alter your self-beliefs or dominate your feelings?

The answer is no. You will be around long after this conflict. You have survived conflict in the past and you will survive it again.

Conflict is temporary. You can rise above it. Second, protect yourself. Make sure that in times of conflict, you increase your self-care routine. Having others be critical of you can be damaging to your self-worth, so do everything you can to counteract that. Be good to yourself. Treat yourself with extra love. Surround yourself with people that make you feel good about yourself. Most importantly, if you have done something wrong, remember that there is a difference between guilt and shame.

Guilt says, "I've done something wrong". **Shame** says, "I *am* something wrong".

Try not to let yourself wander down the shame path. No one is perfect. We all make mistakes. Guilt and remorse simply mean that you are taking responsibility for the mistakes you have made. They should not be a means of placing unnecessarily harsh judgments on yourself. Third, focus on a resolution. Do whatever you can to resolve the conflict. If you need to make an apology, do so. If there is something you could do better from now on, make a resolve within yourself to do so. If you need to have a difficult conversation with someone, encourage yourself to do so if it's going to make things better. Think about the what is needed to make a resolution and carry it out. You might only need to send someone a text or email. You may need to talk to your boss if things at work are upsetting you.

Whatever it is, value yourself enough to do what you can to get to the other side of it. No one needs conflict hovering over their head longterm. Just remember not to put too much pressure on yourself where resolution is concerned if the other person is not receptive to it. It takes two. Sometimes it's just not possible to change the way someone else thinks and feels, so it's important to recognize times when a resolution simply isn't possible. Fourth and finally, let go. Whether the conflict you're experiencing is something that's going to be over by the end of the week or it's more likely to drag on for a long time, practice letting go of things that are out of your control. If you are being treated badly or unfairly by someone, try to rise above it. Don't treat them the same way they are treating you, and don't think of yourself as inferior to them. The fact is, not everyone is going to like you in this world and that is 100% okay.

No one is liked by *everyone*. What other people think of you is none of your business. There have always been bullies in this world and there always will be. Some people treat other people badly just so they can feel better about themselves. That is their problem, not yours. If you have to see someone who treats you poorly on a regular basis, really work on summoning up some inner confidence. Use self-care to maintain feelings of positive self-worth. Talk to a friend who will build you up when you're feeling low. Put on a brave face and practice appearing unshakable when you're in the presence of someone who thinks they're above you. Don't let their issues get under your skin. Remind yourself, when this person is done bullying you, they'll move on to another innocent victim. It's not about you. It's about them.

The last emotionally activating situation I want to discuss are those which cause one to feel like they're *on display*. Here I am referring to things like first dates, job interviews, meeting new people, public speaking… even something as celebratory as getting married or having a surprise birthday party thrown for you. All of these situations are similar in that they place a lot of focus on *you*. And for people who experience social anxiety, being put in a situation where a lot of attention is directed at you can feel downright awful. If you experience panic attacks, situations like these can be major triggers. Having the spotlight on you is rarely something people look forward to when they live with social anxiety. Unfortunately, we can't go through life avoiding the spotlight without having a negative impact on our quality of life.

The fact is, we need people around us. We need the stimulation of meeting new people and broadening our horizons. We need to feel like we can change careers or advance in our chosen career in order to feel hopeful about the future. We need to be celebrated when we're worthy of celebration. We need to step out of our comfort zone in order to keep growing and gaining new strengths. Most importantly, we need to feel comfortable in new and changing environments so that we can get what we want out of life.

There are people in the world who really like being on display and others who don't mind it. If you hate having all eyes on you, it may not be realistic for you to try to become someone who loves attention. But it is possible for you to become someone who simply doesn't mind it. This is something that you can achieve through gradual exposure.

For example, if you apply for five jobs and you get offered an interview for each one, how are you likely to feel during the first interview versus how you'll feel by the fifth? Assuming you'd be happy to get any one of these jobs, chances are, you'll be at your most nervous for the first one and your least nervous by the last. This is because the more you are exposed to that situation, the more you can predict what it's going to be like and the more practice you have being in that type of environment.

So if you have something coming up that's got you feeling anxious, think about some ways you might be able to simulate some gradual exposure. If you've been made best man at your brother's wedding and you're dreading making that speech, start by practicing in front of the mirror. Then ask someone you trust to be your audience in a one-to-one practice session. Then try it in front of a small group of people. Rehearsing is a great way to get yourself used to reciting the speech, but it's also a way for you to get used to feeling nervous. The effects of adrenaline can be a bit dizzying but if you're used to experiencing them, and you're used to pushing through them, you'll be better equipped to cope with them on the big day. The same goes for other types of public speaking, and can even be applied to job interviews and dates.

Is there someone in your life that could help you get comfortable in a strange new experience before you jump into the deep end? Would one of your friends pretend they're interviewing you for a job so you can practice answering questions on the spot?

Could you enlist a friend to go out with you for a pre-date practice session?
Could you visit the place where the date is being held ahead of time so that you know your way around on the night?
Is there something you'd like to bring to your next work meeting that you could run through in front of a mirror or over dinner with your family?

Although it can feel a bit silly at times, rehearsing is a good way to build confidence in daunting situations. Any friends or family members that can provide a safe space and constructive feedback are resources that are worth tapping into.

When life forces you into the spotlight, do your best to embrace it. Remember that it's okay to feel uncomfortable. Nerves are normal. Reach out to someone who cares about you and tell them how you're feeling. Say it before you make that best man speech. Sometimes just getting those words out is enough to take the sting out of anxiety. Do what you can to think rationally.

Ask yourself what's the worst that can happen?
Will this matter in another year?
Is anyone going to remember this next month?
Is this really a big deal?
Have I survived outside my comfort zone in the past?
Am I taking all of this a little too seriously?

Use positive self-talk for slow, rational thinking and logical questions that will help defuse the anxiety. Most importantly, if something in the future is causing you to feel anxious, tell yourself that there is no use worrying about it now. The future and the past are out of reach. Anxiety has no place there. You can worry about it when it happens. Worrying is not going to change the outcome of anything. It will not stop the event from happening; rather it will only stop you from living freely within it. Turn your worry into action where you can. Be as prepared as you can be. But don't worry for the sake of worrying.

This will take practice so try not to be frustrated at the fact that managing anxiety isn't always that simple. All self-progression takes practice and determination. You will get better at it the more you work at it. Keep reminding yourself to stop worrying when you feel future anxiety rising. Do what you can to keep yourself calm and relaxed in the present. Let the future be a point of excitement, not dread. Think about what opportunities may await you. Think about what triumphs you might achieve. Think of a future where anxiety no longer has a hold on you. Toss the negative stuff and the worries to the side. You're worth a life without them.

The Power of Change - Lesson 5

Get yourself in a calm, relaxed state of mind in a quiet, comfortable space. Remove all distractions. Turn off your phone, TV, and computer. Breathe at your own natural pace and close your eyes. Imagine yourself at the triumphant end of your fight with social anxiety. Picture yourself in the most anxiety-inducing situation you can imagine. This can be something real that you expect to happen in the near future or something you just can't imagine being able to do at the present. Picture yourself feeling calm, comfortable, and self-assured. Picture yourself being entirely unshakable. Imagine yourself saying all the right things, smiling naturally, exuding confidence and warmth.

Use this image as a point of hope as you work towards being your best self. Visualize this version of yourself when you need to feel positive about a future event because this is a version of yourself that you can and will eventually be. You are putting in a lot of work right now and it is going to pay off.

How To Talk To Anybody

When it comes to social anxiety, if you lack conversational skills or you constantly worry about how you're coming across, engaging in a conversation can be excruciating. So you might need some practice where talking is concerned in order to kick anxiety for good. Conversations can be overwhelming. Sometimes you're just not quite sure what to say, or the person you're talking to completely misses the point you're trying to make. Other times your jokes don't land or you accidentally offend someone. And, of course, there are the times when you're so nervous that you babble on and on unable to stop yourself or completely freeze up and end up stuck in a painfully awkward silence. The good news is that anyone can learn how to have engaging, enjoyable, successful conversations. Have a look at the following list for some top tips on how to talk to just about anybody.

10 Life-Changing Conversation Skills

1 - Be a great listener.

A lot of times, being a great conversationalist is more about being a good listener than it is about being a good speaker. Sitting in front of someone and talking about yourself for an hour isn't going to make a great impression. It could come across as arrogant and selfish. Rather, people like talking to those who are genuinely interested in what they're saying. They like feeling like what they have to say is important. You can make someone feel valued and respected just by listening to them. So when you're entering a conversation with someone - especially if you're talking to someone you don't know very well or someone you've only just met - enter the conversation primarily as a listener. This way you'll not only show them that you care about what they have to say, but you'll also take some of the pressure off yourself.

Now, although it may be easier to be a good listener than it is to feel like you have to singlehandedly drive a conversation, active listening does not mean just sitting quietly and allowing someone else to do all the talking. If you don't contribute by asking the right questions and showing that you are engaging with the topic at hand, the other person isn't going to have a great time talking to you.

Similarly, if you're too focused on asking a lot of questions but fail to react appropriately to the responses you're given, the person you're talking to is going to feel like they're just being interviewed or put on the spot, not actually having a conversation. The bottom line is that you have to show that you're interested and that you're actually listening. This means reacting appropriately to what the other person is saying and accurately reflecting their feelings back to them. You can also ask further questions encouraging them to elaborate; thus showing that you are interested and engaged.

For instance, imagine someone is telling you that they're getting fed up with things at work. You can reflect their feelings back to them and encourage them to elaborate by saying something like, *"Oh no, that doesn't sound good. What's been going on?"* or *"Work can be so frustrating. How long have you been feeling like this?"* Here you are showing that you are listening and that you care about how they're feeling. The same concept works for positive emotions. Imagine someone tells you that things at work are really good right now and that they just got a raise. You might say something like, *"Wow that's great! How are you going to celebrate?"* or *"Awesome! How did that come about?"*

Notice that in both situations, the tone of the response matches the tone of the other speaker *and* the additional questions give them an opportunity to delve a bit deeper. A good go-to response when someone is telling you about something going on in their lives is to simply ask how they feel about it. Saying something like, *"What was that like for you?"* or *"How are you feeling about that?"* shows that you care while giving them a chance to elaborate. This type of listening makes people feel good. It makes them feel valued and respected. You may be the first person to have asked them how they feel about something they've been wanting to talk about for ages. And when people feel good while talking to you, it makes them want to talk to you more.

Paying close attention as a listener is extremely important. It's easy for people to see when you're not engaged with the topic at hand. And if they get that vibe from you, it could make them feel uncomfortable or embarrassed. The good news is that the more attention you place on someone else, the less attention you'll have to focus on anxiety. It's a win-win.

2 - Note the tone.

There are few things that put people off the way an inappropriate response can. It's easy to get caught up in nerves during a conversation, and if this happens, you might end up missing the point someone is trying to make. They might be telling you something that's really upsetting them, but if you're focusing too much on anxiety rather than actually listening to them, you might accidentally put your foot in your mouth by saying something like, *"that's cool"* or by trying to move onto another topic before they've finished talking. Reacting in the wrong way could really offend or confuse someone while showing that you haven't really been listening, so it's very important to listen and respond appropriately for the tone of the conversation. Think about how you would feel in their shoes. Express empathy. Active listening is a great way to get to know someone and make them feel good in your presence. And the more you really focus on what they are saying, the less likely you are to hear your own anxious thoughts.

Tone is something you should be especially aware of if you're entering a conversation with a group of people. If they're talking about something serious and you enter with a joke, people aren't going to be terribly amused. Similarly, if a group of people is out to blow off steam and have a good time, they're not going to be thrilled if you come in and start talking about things that are overly negative or self-indulgent. They might not want to hear the sad story of your recent break-up if they're trying to celebrate a birthday for instance. It's very important to learn how to read the room. That means taking into consideration whether a conversation is heavy or light, professional or relaxed, formal or informal, and acting appropriately for that situation. Don't disagree just for the sake of it or try to shake things up by being inflammatory or controversial. Group politics are tricky. Unless you are in a group of people whom you know very well, focus on just going along with things. Match your tone to theirs, be respectful of other people's feelings and opinions, and try to take it easy.

When you get good at reading a room, you won't have to try to think up interesting things to say in advance. You won't just be speaking with rehearsed lines or trying to be interesting. Rather, you'll be able to trust your own intuition and ability to blend in by naturally matching the tone of conversations and responding appropriately because you're actively engaged. If this is something you don't feel confident with now, a little practice could go a long way. One way to get better at reading a room is practicing wherever you are without actually joining conversations. For example, you might be sitting in the break room at work and quietly eating your lunch while a few other people are talking. As you eat, listen to what's being said, note the tone, and think about what you might say if you were involved in the conversation. Think about how each speaker is feeling and what they are seeking from their fellow listeners.

Notice if someone says the wrong thing or if someone says something that elicits a positive reaction. You can do this at cafes, the grocery store, the subway, virtually anywhere. Just don't make it obvious that you're eaves dropping!

3 - Ask open questions.

In addition to asking appropriate questions, do your best to avoid closed ones. Closed questions are those that require only a yes or no answer. If you get caught in a loop of asking closed questions, it's possible that your conversational partner is going to feel like they're being interrogated. Furthermore, they won't be giving you anything to actually listen and respond to. If you're only giving them an opportunity to say, *"Yes. No. No. No. Yes. Yes. No,"* how are you going to be able to think of any reaction more interesting than, *"Okay. Cool. Neat. Oh. Hmm."*?

Plus, if you're asking a slue of questions and the other person is only getting to respond with one-word answers, the balance of the conversation is going to be all off. A conversation should be as close to 50/50 as possible in order for everyone to leave feeling good about it. A series of closed questions is going to make for more of a 90/10 conversation. It would feel imbalanced, awkward, and uncomfortable.

If you look back to tip number one where you learned about being a good listener, you'll notice that the example questions are open. Instead of asking *if* someone is going to celebrate their raise, the example asks *how* they're going to celebrate. The example where the person is having a hard time at work steers clear of asking if the person doesn't like their job, but rather focuses on how long the person has been feeling that way and what events led to that feeling. By asking open questions, not only will the other person feel like they're being listened to, but they will also feel like they can relax for a while as you take the lead. If you are involved in a conversation and you notice you're getting a lot of short answers, it may be that the questions you're asking aren't allowing for a more in-depth response.

Generally speaking, sentences that begin with *"Do you"*, *"Have you"*, *"Are you"*, or *"Will you"* are going to be met with closed answers, while sentences beginning with, *"What"*, *"How"*, and

"Why" will invite longer responses. Longer responses will automatically give you more to react to, a clearer view into the tone of the conversation, and a more natural conversational flow. Just be aware that things aren't always straightforward. Sometimes when the other person shuts down and reverts to short answers, it mightn't have to do with your questions. It could be because they don't like the topic at hand or because they find your questions inappropriate.

In this instance, you'll need to fall back on your skills of reading the room so that you can move on to a safer topic that will be more engaging and enjoyable. Steer clear of topics that are private, personal, sexual, or emotionally activating unless you know someone very well or they bring them up themselves. You can easily make someone uncomfortable by being intrusive or crude.

4 - Keep it clean.

This is pretty self-explanatory but worth mentioning. If you have only recently met someone, you're in a professional setting, or you know that someone specifically dislikes profanity or crudeness, avoid using bad language, toilet talk, or talking about things of a sexual nature. Being overfamiliar with someone when you haven't known them for a long time can make them uncomfortable. Certain settings will also require a cleaner choice of topic. Remember to note the tone and read the room. If the other person moves the conversation in that direction and you want to join in, that should be fine. But don't enter a conversation that way unless you are 100% certain that it will be welcome and reciprocated. If you make crass or risqué jokes and no one is laughing, or they're looking around uncomfortably, you've probably crossed a line. All is not necessarily lost but you'll need to guide things back to safer territory asap.

Places and events in which you should pretty much always be on your best behavior include professional or work-related events,

events around children or elderly people, religious environments, quiet venues, formal gatherings and dining experiences, and times when you are a guest in someone else's home. Always keep it clean around bosses, teachers, in-laws, and people you don't know. Just try to keep it respectful.

5 - Don't interrupt.

Once again, this is not a groundbreaking concept but it is one that is well worth mentioning. Interrupting someone is a very good way to show that you're focusing more on talking than listening. I.e. you're focusing on yourself, not them. The fact is, if you are invested in a conversation and you're actually listening and reacting to what the other person is saying and how they're feeling, you are unlikely to interrupt. However, if you're always thinking about what to say next instead of listening to the other person, you're likely to start talking before they've finished. You might even accidentally change the subject before the other person is ready to because you're focusing more on what to say than how to listen. They will pick up on this and may find you to be rude or inconsiderate. If you do accidentally cut someone off, don't worry too much. It happens. Just apologize and ask them to continue with what they were saying.

Whatever you do, don't get caught up in a talk-feud. This is a situation where two or more people are talking at the same time, making it impossible for anyone to listen or get their point across. If someone interrupts you or talks over you, it's important to know when to back down and let them have the stage, even if they were being rude by doing so. At the end of the day, you can only control your own actions. If someone else is being rude, don't rise to it and try to talk over them. Just keep your cool and wait it out.

6 - Don't try too hard.

If you're nervous about talking to people, it's easy to put too much pressure on yourself. You might feel like you have to entertain or impress the other person or pretend to be someone you're not. Maybe you'll agree with everything they say because you want them to like you and you don't want to cause a conflict. Maybe you'll act over familiar with them, sitting too closely, bringing up things that are too personal, or trying to make them laugh by saying things that aren't entirely appropriate for the situation at hand. Perhaps you'll talk too much, interrupt, or rush through the conversation without giving the other person a chance to breathe and relax. You might feel like you have to try to make people laugh so they'll like you, or mimic others to appear more cool.

These are all natural responses to being socially uncomfortable but they are also things that can make you look inauthentic and insecure. The thing is, people can usually see right through you when you're not being your authentic self. They can tell that you are uncomfortable and you may come across as too eager or strange. Trying too hard to make someone like you could also mean inadvertently annoying them, making them uncomfortable, or having them pity you. As I'm sure you're aware, these are not exactly ideal conversational outcomes. What you have to remember is that you aren't in a conversation to impress or entertain anyone. If you go in with that sort of mindset, you're going to find it hard to relax and be yourself. You have to remember that it's okay to slow the pace of a conversation down. Everything you say doesn't have to be a zinger. Moments of silence are okay and totally natural, so try not to fill in every single gap with noise. Don't talk about yourself like you're seeking praise or approval. Focus on asking more questions and offering information about yourself when you're asked for it or when you genuinely have something to contribute because it's relevant to the topic at hand. Always keep in mind that there is no way to make everyone in the world like you. Some people just won't vibe with you and that's totally okay. If you act with dignity and integrity, it won't matter what someone else thinks of you because you'll know in your heart that you were true to yourself.

Remember that rejection is a part of life (*and a topic I will talk more about in Part Three*). Rejection does not define you, nor does it have to be devastating. Try to remind yourself that it's best to surround yourself with people who like and respect the real you. There's no point in building relationships with new people if you're not committed to being yourself when doing so. Otherwise, what's the point? Do your best to relax before conversations with new people and don't put too much pressure on yourself to impress them. If it's someone you're bound to speak to again in the future, use that as a reminder that you don't have to cover all bases in a single conversation.

7 - Be careful with comedy.

Being funny is an amazing quality that can be endearing and magnetic. Being able to make people laugh is truly a gift. But not everyone is blessed with a witty, relatable sense of humor. Some of us are good at making ourselves laugh, or laughing with one or two close friends, but that doesn't necessarily translate into being a natural comedian. When you're talking to new people, or groups of people, you have to be able to notice when your jokes aren't landing. Continuing to make bad jokes is a very easy way to repel people. Reason being, bad jokes can make people uncomfortable. And what's worse, they can make other people feel embarrassed for you. This is not a desirable outcome when hoping to make a good impression. So, remember to keep your eyes and ears open. If you tell a joke, look out for some telltale signs that it is or isn't landing. If people don't laugh, they don't find your joke funny. If they make meek or closed-lip sounds, they're probably uncomfortable. If they're looking around instead of looking at you, they're probably wishing they weren't there. If they fidget or touch their face, neck, or hair, they're not comfortable. If you make a joke for a group of people and they are looking at each other more than they are looking at you, they're not invested in what you're saying.

Remember, you don't have to be entertaining in order for people to like you. Making bad jokes is another way of trying too hard, and it's very easy to see through. Remember too that making fun of people isn't usually a good idea when you've just met them. It's not necessarily going to be thought of as funny. Although some people's sense of humor does lean towards poking fun at their friends and at themselves, if you enter a conversation and just start making fun of people without knowing if it's going to be welcome, it could just seem like you're being rude or that you're socially inept. Most importantly, if you're talking to someone or cracking jokes and they look like they want to leave, let them go! Don't hold people hostage and continue telling them bad jokes. Just relax and bid them farewell.

8 - Know when to change the subject.

In addition to being able to recognize when your jokes aren't landing, it's equally important to notice when the people you're talking to aren't feeling great about subject content of your conversation. Luckily, all the telltale signs listed above are relevant here as well. Fidgeting, looking around, furrowed brows, and half smiles are usually indicative of someone experiencing social discomfort. Groups that look at each other instead of at you is an indication that they feel more comfortable with each other than they do with you. But moments like this happen all the time and they're usually easy enough to recover from. They are not a reason to run away and hide.

Rather, if something you're talking about is making people uncomfortable, just change the subject. Ask someone else a question to take some of the pressure off yourself. Or just let the space breathe for a few seconds and see if someone else will pick up the slack. It's okay to just say something like, "well *that* didn't go down well" and laugh it off. This shows humanity and self-awareness. Making a humorous note of it can help make people feel comfortable again and the conversation could be easily rescued from that point on. Remember that it's okay to make the occasional social faux pas. It's normal to make some conversational mistakes. Everyone does it and it's definitely not the end of the world. In life, we all fall. It's all about how we recover.

9 - Don't talk too fast.

Remember the importance of letting the room breathe and giving the conversation space. In order for the conversation to flow naturally, it has to be evenly paced. Feeling anxious or nervous can cause things to speed up. We may talk too fast, talk without thinking, and even move and breathe too fast. Not only are all of these things visible to the people we're talking to, but they are also distracting, making it harder for you and your listener to focus and think clearly. It's natural to rush when you're nervous. Just do your best to recognize when your mouth is going a mile a minute. You can tell if things are a little too speedy a few ways. The first is that you will feel frantic or even out of breath. Your body may show signs of tension or elation, rather than feeling and appearing relaxed. You may notice that the other person hasn't had many chances to talk. They may be sitting quietly instead of trying to engage with you. Or they may be trying to talk but can't get more than a word or two in because your chatter is taking up all the air space.

Things like this are very common not only for people living with social anxiety, but also for anyone who's feeling uncomfortable or anxious in a situation. None of us feel great about socializing all the time. Everyone experiences social discomfort and conversational reluctance from time to time. So, don't beat yourself up if you notice that you're not doing well in a particular conversation. Self-awareness is the most important thing at the start. If you are aware of your personal struggles, you'll be able to reflect on them and change them with practice.

Take note of things you need to work on and approach them with confidence. We all have limitations, strengths, and weaknesses. Anyone can develop great communication skills so stay hopeful! As always, if you notice that you're running away with the conversation, slow things down by asking some open questions and actively listen as the other person responds. Use this as a method of taking a breather and getting refocussed.

10 - Try to have fun.

Conversations are not supposed to be a form of punishment. They are not designed to make you uncomfortable or under confident. They are not there as a means to be down on yourself or make you feel hopeless. Rather, communication and social stimulation are part of our fundamental needs as human beings. We have an innate need to be part of groups, to feel like we are part of something bigger than ourselves. Socializing helps to connect us to other people. It helps us find likeminded individuals, gives us an opportunity to help and be helped by others, and gives meaning to our lives. Having fun is also a fundamental need. Being able to relax and unwind is an extremely important tool to combat all the serious stuff in life. Work can be hard on us. Relationships can take a toll on us. Keeping up with busy schedules, looking after kids and spouses, trying to thrive in a world that set standards way above the achievable, all of these things are common struggles, but they are also things that many of us cannot escape. So, we need to counteract the effect that all the more weighty things in life have on us. The way we do this is by having fun, connecting with others, and valuing our own need for joy, recreation, and relaxation. Remember that when you are having a conversation with someone, you are not on display. You don't have to seek approval from anyone but yourself. No one has the power to judge you. Not everyone is going to like you, but so what? There isn't a single person on this earth who is liked by everyone. Take comfort in that.

Remember that it is always okay to tell the person you're speaking to that you're feeling nervous. Doing so could reduce the tension that both of you are feeling in that moment. It might be something you can both laugh at. It might create increased feelings of bonding and understanding between you. Above all, know that it is good to be human. You don't have to pretend to be someone you're not. You don't have to pretend to be perfect. People see through that. Everyone has difficulties and struggles. Being open and honest could help someone else do the same. Do your best to seek enjoyment in your conversations. Let go and have some fun whenever you can.

The Power of Change – Lesson 6

Conversations are a lot easier when you have plenty of experience with them. So ask a friend or loved one to rehearse some conversations with you. This can be helpful if you have something like an upcoming job interview, a first date, or a meeting with an old friend that's weighing on your mind. Ask the person you practice with to give you some feedback on your performance. Role play can feel a bit silly or uncomfortable but it's a great way to get used to talking and recovering from conversational mishaps.

Remember that when you're talking to people, you're not always going to come across the way you'd like, so it's important to get used to making some minor mistakes and recovering from them seamlessly. If formal role play isn't for you, just start engaging in conversations in a more natural way. Talk to people whenever you can, and afterwards, take time to reflect on how things went. Think about how you felt both physically and emotionally. Pinpoint any things you could do better next time and make a note of any strengths you have. Recognizing your strong points is extremely important for your self-esteem and confidence, so do not use this exercise to simply point out all the things you did wrong. Always give yourself credit for the things you did right, no matter how small. The more practice you get, the more comfortable conversations are going to be in the future so get out there and start talking!

Quickly Become an Expert in Body Language

Body language is one of the most important elements of communication. When we talk to people, it's not just what comes out of our mouths that influences how someone feels in our presence. It is not only our words that do the talking. Rather, it has been said that a mere 7% of communication is verbal. This means that a shockingly monumental 93% of communication is non-verbal. Think about how significant that is. 93% of what we *say* to each other is wordless. The way we hold ourselves and position our bodies during a conversation says a lot about how we're feeling. We tell a lot about ourselves by how we position ourselves in a room, how we hold our bodies, what we do with our hands, even the pace of our breath.

Like most animals, humans adopt a number of natural postures designed to communicate messages without speaking. These range from the most simple signals like smiling, laughing, and frowning to those far more complex messages that come from things like body positioning, voluntary and involuntary hand movements, and a wide array of types of eye contact. And what's more, none of these forms of non-verbal communication can be taken at face value. In fact, it is how they overlap and work together that reveals the whole story. For instance, smiling doesn't always mean that someone is having a good time.

As you read in the last section, someone who is uncomfortable in a social situation may smile in an attempt to hide their discomfort. In a case like this that person's smile may be undermined by their body positioning. They may be facing the door instead of facing the person they're talking to. Their hand and arm movements may send signals that are in direct conflict with their smile. For instance, they may cross their arms or play with their hair rather than letting their limbs rest. Their eye contact may be shifty or nonexistent, signaling a desire to get away from the topic or the conversation completely. Needless to say, body language is not always straightforward. But many times it is. Learning the basics of both sending and receiving non-verbal communication and learning to trust your instincts will help you decipher what's happening socially if you tend to misinterpret human subtleties.

Body language isn't something that most people actively think about. It's something that usually falls under the radar, and that happens subconsciously. There are many people in the world who simply have a natural instinct when it comes to reading and displaying bodily signals. Their ability to read the room is likely to be a major strength when it comes to existing in the social sphere. If you possess this strength, consider yourself lucky. This will make things easier for you, even if social anxiety gets the better of you now and again.

There are also plenty of people in the world who find body language and other non-verbal communication to be quite mysterious. They can't always read what's being communicated by facial expressions. They might be oblivious to subtle changes in body positioning. And if you fall into this category, this section should be quite helpful. Remember that there are also plenty of people that fall somewhere in the middle. You might have pretty decent instincts but a lack of knowledge about some of the smaller ways people communicate silently.

Think of body language just like you think about verbal communication. There are always two elements of a conversation working in tandem: What is said, and what is unsaid. If communication were a bicycle, body language would be the front wheel, while spoken words would be the back. Very few of us are skilled enough to ride a unicycle, so it's important that we can both understand and rely on both wheels. When it comes to getting your point across, knowing what to *say* verbally is as important as knowing what to *do* physically. And in addition to understanding how to *speak* to others with body language, we must also get good at *listening* to the body language of others. In verbal communication, we know that listening involves sharing the audible space in the room, reacting appropriately to what is said, and asking questions to make the other person feel valued.

Listening to *non*-verbal communication is more about picking up on subconscious clues, understanding why someone's body is positioned the way it is, paying attention to shifts in facial expression, and displaying positions of empathy to show that you are paying attention. So as you can tell, when we talk about learning the art of body language, we're not just talking about sending out the right messages with our bodies. We're also talking about picking up on other people's signals and responding to them appropriately.

For instance, if you are accidentally adopting positions that make you appear standoffish, uninterested, or uncomfortable while having a conversation with someone, they will probably pick up on this to some degree. Now, this isn't something to become completely preoccupied with. The aim here is not to add to your anxiety! But learning and perfecting some basic body language skills could help you better understand the unwritten rules of socialization, gain confidence in the social sphere, and have more successful communications all around.

The following list will break down the most important elements of body language. Think about these things in light of both speaking and listening. What is your body language telling other people? What is their body language telling you?

The 5 Powerful Stages of Body Language

<u>1 - Body Positioning</u>

The way we position our body says a lot about how we're feeling. It can tell someone if we're comfortable or uncomfortable, interested or disinterested, open or on guard. In addition to all of that, the way we position our bodies can also have an impact on how the person we're talking to feels. Think about what it feels like to be standing in line at the grocery store. Imagine that the person behind you is standing very close to you. This might force you to stand even closer to the person in front of you. Being in close quarters with strangers in this single file manner can be physically and emotionally uncomfortable. Now think about standing in an elevator with strangers. Have you ever noticed that if you are standing in close proximity to a stranger side-by-side, it feels less intense than if they were standing directly in front of or behind you?

You might still wish you weren't forced to be so close to a stranger but the feeling of pressure is usually significantly reduced when standing side-by-side than it is when you are in a single file line. Try lining up with two friends or family members to test this out. First stand close to each other in a single file line. Then stand side-by-side. Note any feelings of threat or discomfort you experience in the first position. Then see how much of that pressure is relieved when your friends move to the side of you. This phenomenon is something you can use to your advantage when you're deciding where to sit or stand when conversing with someone. Facing someone directly can be off-putting. It can feel intrusive and demanding. So, sitting across from someone with your shoulders squared to them might make them feel like they're being put on the spot. It could also make *you* feel like *you're* being put on the spot.

Conversely, positioning yourself at a 45 degree angle from your conversational partner, that is to say, placing yourself so that you are halfway between facing them directly and being beside them, is the ideal positioning for a comfortable conversation. This is a non-threatening, relaxed position. Remember not to sit or stand too closely to someone. A two to three foot distance is ideal. Over the next few weeks or so, look at the world with this theory in mind. Think about where you might sit if you were talking to someone in various locations.

Where would be the best place for a conversation in the break room at work?
Where would you sit if you were meeting someone in a cafe?
Take note of how you feel when being placed in various positions by other people.
How does it feel when someone approaches you squarely and face-to-face?
Do you feel better facing slightly towards someone on a bench or sitting on opposite sides of a table facing them head-on?
How does it feel when someone stands too close to you?

Body positioning is not just important when deciding where to sit or stand. It also includes a variety of subtleties. For instance, when we are interested in what someone is saying, when we feel comfortable with them, or when we're listening intently, we lean in, towards them. Doing this physically shows that we are engaged with what they are saying. When we are uncomfortable, uninterested, or feel superior to someone, we lean back, away from them. This is something to keep in mind when positioning your own body, but it's also a good way to understanding how the person you're talking to is feeling.

Similarly, the way our feet, legs, and shoulders are directed also tells a lot about how we're feeling. Facing our feet or shoulders towards someone, or crossing our legs towards them, usually shows that we are happy in their presence. Facing our feet, shoulders, or legs away from someone, or facing them towards the door means that we are probably not enjoying or invested in the conversation and that we'd like to get away. Practice reading body language when you are out in public or even at home or work. Watch other people as they converse and think about the direction they are facing. Try to interpret the silent signals they are sending each other. When you are talking to someone you're comfortable with, think about your own body language and what it is subconsciously communicating on your behalf. Remember, self awareness is the foundation of positive change. Get to know the way your body speaks so that you can better control it and use it to your advantage.

2 - Signs of tension and distress

There are quite a few ways humans express negative emotion non-verbally. Visible tension can be seen in the jaw, neck, and shoulders. You may see someone's shoulders become slightly raised as tension increases or notice that they are clenching their jaw and neck muscles. Crossing one's arms also tends to signify that someone is emotionally *"closed for business"*. They may be unhappy, wary, guarded, or judgmental of the person they're speaking to. This is a position to be very careful with when you are talking to other people as well. Yes, crossing your arms might feel comfortable for you physically, but it can be perceived by others as a move of dominance, annoyance, impatience, and judgement.

Touching one's face, neck, shoulders, and hair a lot is another classic sign of distress. Humans have a large amount of nerve endings in their head and shoulders. Rubbing one's face and neck, touching one's scalp and shoulders a lot, or constantly fixing one's hair is often a subconscious way of self soothing. If you notice your conversational partner compulsively touching these areas, it could mean that they aren't feeling comfortable. Likewise, if you find yourself doing this when you're talking to someone, they could be perceiving you as being uncomfortable or anxious.

Finally, positions and movements that physically block one's heart signify defensiveness and feelings of threat. This is usually quite subtle and you may not pick up on it unless you're looking for it. Chest blocking may be done by the crossing of arms, but it is often done even less obviously.

For instance, the person you're talking to may hold their coffee cup close to or in front of their heart. They may hold their sweater or bag in front of their chest like a shield or barrier. They may twist their upper body so that a shoulder blocks the line between you and their chest. Look out for moves like this and try to be aware of any subconscious signals you may be displaying unintentionally. Try to adopt an open position with your chest. This shows that you have dropped your guard and are inviting the other person to relax and do the same. Be careful not to over-interpret moves that cover or cross the chest. Keep in mind that some people gesticulate a lot without meaning or purpose. And this does not necessarily mean that they are feeling threatened or guarded. Remember too, that if you are saying something that is particularly shocking or emotional, the other person may place a hand on their chest as a response. This is not a sign of discomfort, but rather a sign of empathy. Remember that although the heart is generally thought of as subconsciously signifying a place of vulnerability, it is also a place associated with strong emotion.

Over the next few days take note of how you subconsciously protect or draw attention to your heart. Notice what type of position you're in when you're at your most uncomfortable, and see how many times you place a hand on your chest when gasping in shock. All of this is related to your own subconscious awareness of the position of your heart.

3 - Eye contact and facial expressions
Eye contact is something a lot of people are uncomfortable with. This is becoming increasingly true as human communication moves away from the physical world and towards faceless, written communication via email, text and social media. The thing is, when people actively think about making eye contact, they often go too far. For instance, yes, it may be considered strange or rude to make no eye contact at all. But it may also be off-putting to make too much eye contact. The general rule is that you should make eye contact during about 70% of your conversation. Giving 100% eye contact during a conversation could really freak somebody out. Try it out with a friend and have them do the same to you. It doesn't feel good. Instead, think of it

as 70/30. 70% of the time, you should be making eye contact to show that you're engaged. Don't open your eyes too wide or stare. Don't look too intensely into someone else's eyes. Exaggerated eye contact like that can make people feel like you're trying to look right through them. Just let your gaze relax and take in their whole face.

The other 30% of the time, you should be looking somewhere else. The safest places to look are slightly down or slightly away at an angle. Try not to look out a window or watch other things going on around you as this will make it seem as though you aren't paying attention or could make you look like you're bored. Looking up is okay if you're thinking, but it can be a sign of distraction if you're not. If at any time you notice your conversational partner following your gaze - for instance looking up when you do or looking over their own shoulder when you're looking in that direction - they're getting a signal that you're distracted and looking at something of specific interest outside the conversation. This is why slight eye movements and a more relaxed gaze are more effective. They are more natural movements and unlikely to steal any attention away from the conversation.

A slow blink is a good way to reduce eye contact without appearing like you're looking away intentionally. Closing your eyes for a moment and nodding slowly shows that you are actively engaged and listening intently.

Facial expressions are also important. Generally speaking, your face should look relaxed, not tensed up. It should also display empathy. The facial expressions people make while they are listening to someone else talk should reflect the tone of the conversation. Tilt your head slightly to show sympathy, confusion, or an interest to hear more. If someone is telling you something crazy that happened to them, match the look of shock on their face with your own. If they're telling you something difficult, sad, or sombre, reflect that back to them facially.

Basically, try to match your face to theirs to show that you are listening to what they're saying and that you are in agreement with their feelings on the matter. Just try not to make it too obvious and don't do it 100% of the time. You don't want to look like you're jokingly mimicking or mocking them. Trust your own face to express how you're feeling in regards to what you're hearing. Most of this will happen automatically.

4 - What to do with your hands

What we do with our hands when we're talking and listening can say a lot about how we're feeling. When we are relaxed in a conversation, we will naturally adopt an open position. Our hands will rest lightly on the table or in our laps. Our arms will not be crossed or covering our hearts. When we are not relaxed, we fidget. We may hold props over our chest, change position constantly, touch our face and neck, fold or scrunch bits of tissue or paper, drum our fingers on the table, crack our knuckles, or bite our fingernails. The hands are a very expressive tool. People who are unsettled in a conversation might do things that involve reaching away from it.

For instance, they may grab onto other chairs that are out to the side or behind them. They may move their bag multiple times, move things around on the table, mess with one of their shoe laces, or brush invisible crumbs off their clothing. These are all signs that something isn't quite right. Often, moves like these are habitual rather than emotional so don't get too hung up on them. But do be aware of them, and definitely be aware of what your own hands are saying when you're talking to people. Try to keep your shoulders, arms, and hands relaxed. Practice this whenever you're talking to someone you feel comfortable with. Notice where your hands want to go and try to retrain them if you tend to fidget a lot. Do your very best to keep your hands out of your mouth. Biting your nails or the skin on your fingers is a serious sign of distress and it can make other people uncomfortable and even grossed out.

Be conscious of things like receipts and wrappers. Throw them away if you're likely to subconsciously fold or twist them while you're talking to someone. Practice having slow, steady, silent hands if you want to appear relaxed and at ease.

5 - Empathy positioning
Empathy is something that is often expressed non-verbally. We don't always have to tell someone that we understand how they're feeling in order to get the point across. Rather, we do so by mirroring. Mirroring means to change one's own body positioning to match someone else's. For instance, above I spoke about changing your facial expression to match someone else's to show that you feel for them. This is same theory on a larger scale. If you think about this periodically throughout a conversation with a close friend, you might notice that both of you are sitting the same way without even thinking about it. You may both have an elbow on the table, propping your head up with one hand. You may both have one hand on your hip, or you may be both facing towards or away from something in particular.

Again, this is something that usually happens without a second thought but if you recognize that your body doesn't do this automatically, it may be helpful to employ mirroring in some circumstances. Obviously, you don't want to *constantly* mirror the person you're talking to. If you do, they're likely to think you're involved in some sort of dare or joke, or that you're running through some exercise you learned in a high school drama class. Rather, when the person you're talking to says something that is very important to them, you can show that you care by slowly shifting to match their position. If they tilt or lower their head when telling you about something that's upsetting them, doing the same can signify solidarity. If they're feeling tense about something and it shows in their shoulders, you may display some slight tension in your own upper body.

Before you go out in the world to try this out, see if you can notice other people unconsciously mirroring your body positions.

Note especially times when you are displaying tension and another person mirrors that back to you. That can be a signifier of the type of energy you're bringing into a conversation.

Remember that a lot of these things will come naturally to you to some extent. You may just need to become more aware of them so that you can read the tone of conversations more accurately. Try not to become preoccupied with body language as it could get in the way of really listening to people. Just be aware of these basics and think about anything you'd like to address in particular. Remember the aim is not to become a conversational robot, it's simply to appear more at ease in the social world.

The Power of Change - Lesson 7

Stand or sit on a chair in front of the mirror and practice portraying a relaxed and engaged position. Relax your shoulders, tilt your head slightly as though you are listening intently. Soften your facial expression and allow your hands to rest lightly in your lap or at your side. Try expressing a number of emotions using only non-verbal communication. Try to express discomfort or tension. Express frustration or anger. Express sympathy and sadness. Express anxiety followed by relaxation. Think about all the ways your body changes when you talk to other people.

When you find a position that you feel makes you appear to be relaxed, try it out on a friend. Try to actively read what other people's bodies are saying about them. The more you practice things like this, the more you will be able to rely on your skills in situations that you find particularly activating. Doing this will give you a greater sense of control in surroundings that would usually cause you to feel a rise in anxiety.

Essential Skills for Life Online

We all know that text-based communication is a big part of life in today's society. Most people keep up with multiple social media accounts on a daily basis linking them to everyone they know plus a bunch of people they've never even met. Even those of us who do not indulge in social media to its greatest extent still communicate to others via text and email. Online dating and online job recruitment are becoming more and more common as time goes by. Let's face it, more and more real-life activities are being replaced by online versions every day.

For someone living with social anxiety, life online can be especially attractive as it often feels *"safer"* than socializing in person. Text based communication gives us time to think about our responses. It puts a wall between us and the people we're talking to. They can't see our face and therefore they cannot know our true feelings. Social media gives us an opportunity to present what we believe to be our best selves. We show the world what we want it to see and hide the rest. We have some control over how we will be perceived by others. And we can do all of these things without ever leaving our comfort zone. We don't even have to get dressed. We don't have to face large crowds or go places we don't like. We rarely have to look anyone in the eye. But regardless of how safe life online can feel, it is not without its dangers.

Becoming too comfortable socializing online can make you more reluctant to socialize in person. If you experience feelings of *"safety"* when you're online, you could be inadvertently causing yourself feel *unsafe* in the physical world, thus worsening social anxiety. The fact is, there are a lot of people in the world whose experiences with social anxiety have sprung directly from their overuse of social media and text-based communication. Doing most of all of your socializing online simply means being out of practice when it comes to actual face-to-face communication. It's a common method of avoidance. Most people would agree that as a society, we are becoming increasingly socially awkward the more life online replaces physical, face-to-face social interaction. And the thing is, there are plenty of anxiety triggers online as well. It's something that needs to be addressed.

Is social media all bad? No. For most people, it's just a part of life. But life online does come with a different set of rules. It possesses different pros and cons and therefore poses different obstacles. Yes, socializing online can keep us connected to people. We can connect with likeminded individuals and carry on conversations without disruption to any plans or obligations we have in the physical world. We can get things done faster in the workplace. We can keep in touch with people who live far away. But life online can breakdown boundaries that are important for all of our emotional safety. It makes us contactable all the time. We are constantly connected to everyone we know. It can be hard to get a break from it all. People can message us any time, day or night, and we're expected to reply in a timely manner.

That's a lot of unnecessary pressure to be put under. In addition, the tone of the written word is not always easy to decipher. If you've ever dated someone online or experienced a conflict with someone via text, have you ever had to show an outside party a message from that person because you couldn't entirely figure out what it meant? Have you ever received mixed signals from someone online? Most people have, and this is usually down to the lack of boundaries there are for life online and the ambiguous nature of the written word. Jokes can be taken as serious. Lines get crossed. A message that is too direct can read as rude. One with too many emojis will appear unprofessional. The line between personal and professional may become blurry. Texting or emailing while drunk can cause a slue of misunderstandings. Texting too often makes you look too eager, not texting enough makes you seem uninterested. It doesn't take a rocket scientist to recognize that even if you enjoy life online, it isn't without its shortcomings.

One of the biggest difficulties of living too much of our lives online - especially if we live with social anxiety - is that it's too tempting to use it as a substitute for real life interaction. Online dating, for instance, cannot act as a complete substitute for finding the right mate in the physical world. It can be successfully used to meet someone new, but it shouldn't be used to conduct an entire relationship without actually meeting someone in person. We have to know when it's time to meet someone in real life or walk away completely. Likewise, we have to be able to recognize when we're using social media or other text-based communications as a means of avoidance. Chatting to people online cannot be used as a substitute for human contact, no matter how effective it is, how much easier it feels, or how meaningful it may seem. We all have a fundamental need to connect with each other in the physical world. There is no substitute for that.

Perhaps the biggest danger of life online is the fact that it can have dramatic effects on your self-esteem. You can be up one day and down the next, and all just because of a few clicks. When you post something about yourself online, you are putting yourself out there to be judged. You may be approved of or rejected by such a thoughtless action as the click of a mouse. If you place too much importance on how many "likes" you get, you're entering dangerous territory. What if no one likes, approves of, or celebrates something you were really proud of? What if they just scroll right by it without giving it a second thought? It can hurt. It can make you doubt yourself.

It can take the wind out of your sails. You may even delete the post so that you can hide or forget about those 5 measly "likes" you got because their mere existence is painful. But the fact is, "likes" should never be given the power to dictate how you feel about yourself at any given time. Most people scroll through social media without even stopping for a second glance. Pressing the "like" button, or not pressing it, is often a thoughtless gesture. People don't think deeply about everything they "like" and don't "like". They're usually just scrolling and tapping, scrolling and tapping. Yet if too many people scroll without tapping, it can feel like you've been rejected by literally everyone you know. You assume that even people who may not have actually seen your post have purposefully not "liked" it. It's dangerous. And by the same rite, if one of your posts harvests a ton of "likes", you could feel amazing about yourself the whole day.

My point is that this is very flimsy ground for your self-esteem to reside on. It's dangerous territory if you're already under confident or suffer from feelings of low self-worth. If you don't already love and approve of yourself, putting yourself out there on the internet is a bold move. The fact is, it is far to easy to feel rejected via your cell phone.

The thing is, life online is unavoidable for most people. Some people love social media. They genuinely enjoy technology and the feelings of connectivity they get when they're online. But even those of us who are more measured with our time online or who shy away from social media completely are still involved with emailing and texting. It's all just a part of life now. So how can we all live a healthy life online? Have a look at this list of Do's and Don'ts to keep you right.

Staying Safe Online

DO:
- Stay in touch with family and friends who you rarely have the opportunity to see in person.
- Use text and email to set up meetings and other arrangements.
- Use text and email to talk about things of limited importance.
- Use social media to get involved with groups who have the same values as you, both locally and afar.
- Use social media and online dating to meet new people.
- Use social media or email as a first point of contact if you meet someone new and aren't ready to share your phone number with them right away.
- Find people you've lost touch with online and reconnect with them.

- Update people on the goings on in your life if you can do so without setting yourself up for approval or rejection.
- Be a part of your community by sharing locally relevant posts such as lost pets or crime watch.

<u>Set some boundaries</u>.
- Decide on a cut off time each night so that you don't find yourself messaging someone when you should be relaxing.
- In the beginning of a new relationship, only text as much as you would normally like to.
- If you start a relationship by being available all the time, people will expect that of you for the durations of the relationship.
- Don't be strong armed into having important conversations via text if you don't want to.
- Think about setting some rules that will make you happier when it comes to messaging people in general.
- Limit the amount of time you spend online.

DON'T:
- Don't use social media as a way to present a different or preferable version of yourself. Be proud of who you really are!
- Don't use it to stalk people you have broken up with or used to be friends with. Stalking is a behavior that usually precedes bad feelings, obsessive negative thinking, and relationship breakdowns. Never stalk someone you know, even if they're dating your ex. It's inappropriate and unkind.
- Don't use social media to check up on the person you are currently dating. Don't look through their *"likes"* or take note of who is *"liking"* their posts.
- Never ever read someone's private texts or emails. Trust is extremely important in relationships.
- Checking up on your partner online is *actively* doubting them and being suspicious of their intentions. Speak to them directly if you want answers.

- Don't use social media as a means to boost your self-esteem. Good feelings about yourself should come from within as well as experiences you have in the real world with people who are in your life in the physical sense. Positive feelings that come from "likes" are fleeting.

- Don't compare yourself to other people. People have a tendency to hide their bad qualities online. They present versions of themselves that make them look like they have everything they could ever want. But believing that is a trap. The fact is, everyone has problems. No one's life is ever as perfect as it may seem online. Don't hurt yourself by wishing you had what other people appear to have.

- Don't use life online as a means to avoid real life socializing.
- Don't use it as a means to attract attention. Writing a lot of negative or self-pitying posts can get annoying for your friends. Try not to use social media as a place to vent all your frustrations. It could make you appear desperate, needy, and overly negative.
- Don't use it to actively dislike or criticize people. Hatred is ugly and can be toxic and addictive. If you are using social media as a place to judge other people, stop doing that. Unfriend someone if you don't like them. Don't actively seek out people just so you can hate-view them. It's a waste of time and will not lead to any truly positive or peaceful feelings.

- Don't use social media to "hide" in public. This means keeping tabs on people and being overly curious about what specific people are up to without them knowing you're watching.
- Don't share too much about yourself online. Keep things that are personal close to your chest. It's important to value your own privacy. Remember to maintain your integrity and dignity. If you want to confide in someone about something that's on your mind, choose someone you trust rather than going public with it right away. Self-protection is important. Remember that anything you put online could very well be there forever, so use caution when sharing.

- Don't hound people or message them constantly. It can be annoying for people to feel like you're always texting them.

Everyone needs space, so make sure you're coming up for air regularly. Being constantly available can make you appear needy and making yourself constantly available for someone is not healthy for either of you. Maintain your autonomy and trust that if a relationship is meant to be, it will be.

- Don't over-analyze texts and emails trying to find hidden meaning. If you're not sure what someone means in a message, ask them directly.
- Don't hold onto communications that were painful. Rereading painful messages is not being kind to yourself. Old text and emails don't mean anything after a while. Reminding yourself of old conflicts or of better times is a means of emotional self-harm. Delete emotionally activating messages to protect yourself.
- Don't get into fights online. If you are feeling extreme feelings of negativity, step away from the computer. Remember that if you say something harsh, it could be there forever. Other people could see you at your worst. Take a deep breath and relax for a while. If you still feel passionately later, think about how best to express that when you've calmed down a little bit.

One final thing worth mentioning is knowing how to recognize if you have a social media addiction. It's important to know when you need to take a break. If you are constantly online or attached to your cell phone 24/7, you might need to get a little space from it. If your self-esteem or your mood is too closely attached to what's happening on your phone, that's a good indication that something needs to change. If you're constantly checking to see when someone is online or whether or not they have read your messages, you may be looking at things in an unhealthy light. Remember that everyone has their own lives. Many times when someone doesn't respond to your messages right away it's just because they're busy. It's not necessarily about you. But if you have an addiction to life online, a message that goes unanswered can be devastating. So too, if perusing social media is filling you with negative feelings, chances are, you need a break. Feeling angry or annoyed after being online is an indication that you need to step away. Feeling low or inferior to others is another. Feeling frustrated, lonely, jealous, devastated, disappointed, or depressed are a few more. The same goes for text conversations that are negative, cyclical, pointless, and emotionally harmful. Know when to step away.

So, what can you do if you feel like life online is getting the better of you? First of all, boundaries must be put in place. You have to know when to stop replying to someone and when to stop checking for new messages. Sometimes, you might have to actively give your phone to someone else and have them hide it for the day in order to give yourself some peace. We have to be able to get space from the things that are triggering us. Sometimes physically separating yourself from your phone is the best way to do this. Take a walk and leave the phone at home. Be realistic if your phone is having a negative effect on you and value yourself enough to protect yourself from it. If social media addiction is the problem, start by checking how much time you're spending online. Most cell phones have the ability to show you how much of your time is being eaten up by social media, texting, and emailing.

Be honest with yourself if yours has gotten out of control. Think about how much you'd like to reduce your usage by, and keep close track of yourself. If there is something you've been doing online that you know is problematic, make a resolve to stop doing it and move past it. If you feel like you are addicted to life online and it is having a seriously negative effect on you or your relationships with others, consider taking an extended break from all social media. Log out of all your accounts and remove the apps from your phone to avoid temptation. You can always go back at a later date, but once you get through the first few days, it will get easier. You may find a significant improvement in your mood, your levels of anxiety, your sleep cycle, and in fact, you may find yourself with a lot more time on your hands to do other things.

Taking a break from social media is also a fantastic way to force yourself back into the physical world. Instead of messaging someone online, you might reach out to them directly and arrange a coffee date. This means that your real-life relationships will get stronger and I guarantee that your self-esteem will as well.

Online dating is another thing that has the potential to be seriously addictive. If you have been dating or chatting to multiple people for an extended period of time, take some time to think about why this is. Are you actually looking for someone special or are you just killing time? Are you remaining in multiple half-relationships because you're scared of entering one special one? Are you involved with online dating because you're bored? If so, is that fair to the people you're talking to? Are you using online dating as a way to remain busy, thus avoiding your own thoughts or pain? Is online dating having a positive effect on your life or is it just serving as a distraction?

Being honest with yourself is extremely important when it comes to facing up to addiction. If you think things have gotten a little out of control, try to grab hold of the reins. Stop giving all your love and attention to your cell phone and start taking it back for yourself. If life online has become a way for you to stay busy in order to ignore your more difficult feelings, it might be time to take a break and start working through the stuff that's bothering you.

Remember that a quiet mind is a healthy mind. If you struggle to sit and be quiet for longer than a few minutes, it's possible that by staying busy and staying stimulated, you're actually running away from thoughts and feelings that need your attention. These things will not go away on their own. Try to give yourself some space to listen to yourself and some time to heal. Life online will always be there so you can go back again in a little while if you want to. Just make sure that you're prioritizing your own emotional wellbeing above all.

The Power of Change – Lesson 8

In order to find out how life online is affecting you, try keeping a journal for one week. Write down how you feel after social media sessions, or after text-based conversations. Ideally, you should write down your feelings after every online experience you have, but if this seems like too much, just do it each evening before you go to bed. In your journal you don't have to write down all the specifics. What matters are the *feelings*.

Do you feel exhausted by it?
Sad?
Elated?
Angry or frustrated?
Good about yourself?
Bad about yourself?
Anxious or nervous?
Uncertain or confused?

Be honest and write down whatever it is that you feel as a direct effect of life online. At the end of the week, look at your journal and see if you can identify any problems. Are you often low after being online? Does your mood change constantly as a result of positive and negative stimulation online? Is your self-esteem directly affected by what's happening online? Be realistic with your conclusions and think about any ways you can improve how you feel by altering the way you use life online.

Part Three: Having Control & Power Over Your Own Life

As I expressed at the beginning of this book, this final section is going to very briefly touch upon the wider spectrum of how social anxiety has affected you. Your self-esteem and your relationships with others are important things to assess and think about while embarking on any journey of self-development. As such, you will find that this section is more concise than Parts One and Two. The hard work has already been done. So just think of Part Three as my final thoughts to you as you near the end of this particular part of your journey, just a few things to think about as you reach further into your future. It is designed to be read when you feel that you've got a better handle on social anxiety, so don't rush into it if you don't feel like you're ready just yet.

Hopefully the first two parts of this book will have left you feeling more knowledgeable, motivated, and eager to continue bettering your life experiences. Hopefully you are already starting to notice that you're thinking differently and taking better care of yourself. Hopefully you are seeing an improvement in how you were feeling before you began this journey. This next section can be read at your leisure. It may be used to compliment what you worked on in Parts One and Two, or it may be used to spur you on to further personal development in the future.

How to *Actually* Improve Your Self Esteem

As you've learned throughout this book, it is impossible to focus on self-development without taking our self-esteem into consideration. This is a part of us that is connected to everything we do, how we feel, and how we interact with the world around us. Self-esteem is often at the root of the things we struggle with the most. It also has a way of getting us caught in cycles of negative feelings and experiences. If our self-esteem is poor, we are more likely to be affected by social anxiety. And likewise, the more we struggle with anxiety, the worse our self-esteem will become. We may become angry at ourselves and get into the habit of judging ourselves harshly. We might develop harmful self-beliefs, like insisting that we're different from other people, feeling like we'll never being able to fit in, believing we'll never being able to have a *"normal life"* or that we'll always be the underdog. It's easy to lose hope when life becomes difficult. The longer we live with limitations like social anxiety, the harder it gets to imagine life getting better.

Plus, the more we struggle in life, the more likely we are to become bitter or resentful of others. It's easy to develop a chip on your shoulder when it always feels like everyone else has it easier than you do. But you have to know and believe that social anxiety does not have to be a lifelong diagnosis. As I've stressed from the beginning, social anxiety is not part of who you are. It is not your identity. The more you do to care for yourself, to show yourself love, kindness, and forgiveness, the closer you'll be to being free from anxiety for good.

The fact is, we need to have a healthy self-esteem to get through the many obstacles life will throw at us. We need to be able to judge ourselves realistically and positively. We need to be strong enough to get back up each time we get knocked down. Because that is the nature of life. No one can live happily with low self-esteem, but it's up to us to pull ourselves back up again when we fall.

Low self-esteem and poor self-confidence can be huge dampeners in our lives. They can hold us back from trying new things, taking risks, building new relationships and fixing broken ones, standing up for ourselves, and believing that we deserve more. They can hold us back from attempting to accomplish things just because we're afraid of how failure may affect us. They can force us to avoid putting ourselves out there romantically, applying for new jobs, getting involved with local groups and events that we'd really like to be a part of otherwise. They are a vital part of our emotional wellbeing. But they are fragile. They are things we have to be careful with. Things we must value enough to protect through life's many ups and downs. Because the more we hold ourselves back, the more we are telling ourselves that we're not good enough and that we cannot succeed. We have to believe in ourselves. We have to be able to live with the belief that we can achieve what we want to achieve. We have to be able to look at our own unique personal skills and qualities and view them with kindness, generosity, love, and honesty. We have to learn to see the good in ourselves and approve of ourselves, because no one else is obligated to that for us.

One of the most powerful things we can do to start strengthening our self-esteem is to vow to judge ourselves realistically and by our own standards. This means putting an end to negative self-talk. It means not beating ourselves up when we don't do the best at something. But most importantly, it means being able to look at our actions and reactions with a clear head. It means treating ourselves like a friend. So, if you hear yourself putting yourself down, discounting your accomplishments, or noticing every tiny little negative thing without giving yourself credit for any of the positive stuff, make a vow to turn that around. Instead of pointing out all the things you could've done better, big up the things you did well. Mistakes and shortcomings are a part of life. If there is something you could've done better, you can do better at it next time.

For now, you have to take note of the things you're doing well. You have to say, *"Well maybe I didn't reach the goal I was shooting for, but I did take a few steps towards it. I did better than I could've a year ago. I did better than I thought I could at all. I've made some progress."*

Remember this: Self approval is the antidote to rejection and feelings of low self-worth. We have to be our own cheerleaders in life, and I know that that's no easy feat if you've been down on yourself for a while. But all it takes is practice. You have to remember to find the good in everything you do.

So what if you failed? What did you accomplish on the way?
So what if you fell? Didn't you get back up?
So what if you cried all night after a hard day at work. You went back in the next day anyway.

What did you do that's worth your own praise and approval? Judge yourself by your own standards and your own criteria. What do you value? Did you live up to that? That's what really matters.

Who cares if what you accomplished would be easy for someone else? Who cares if no one else would praise you for something so seemingly insignificant? Healthy self-esteem doesn't come from comparing ourselves to other people. It doesn't come from judging ourselves the way other people may judge us. It comes from recognizing our own strengths and noting our own progress. We have to get good at recognizing the little things, offering ourselves praise every single time we do something better than we could have in the past, and indulging in daily self-care practices. When you judge yourself and your accomplishments, take into consideration your own standards. Maybe you didn't meet someone else's standards, but did you live up to your own? Were you true to your own values and ideals? Did you act according to what is most important to *you*? If so, give yourself credit for it.

Self-doubt and self-criticism are addictive. Negative thinking can become habitual. If you become used to putting yourself down or always seeing the worst in yourself, you're going to have to do something to change that. You have to start challenging your negative self-beliefs with logical, realistic thinking. A good way to do this is by first recognizing when your thoughts are negative. As soon as you notice your thoughts going into negative territory, combat them by thinking of a specific positive example to the contrary.

For instance, let's say you ran into an old friend at the grocery store and you were a bit flustered throughout the conversation because you weren't expecting to see them. You could easily beat yourself up for not being your best self in that moment. But instead of doing that, you could focus on something positive and specific. Perhaps you remained in that conversation even though you wanted to make your excuses and run away. Perhaps you saw that person from across the room and instead of hiding behind a display of cookies, you were brave enough to approach them and say hello. Perhaps you said something that made them laugh. Maybe just the fact that you survived the conversation is enough to pat yourself on the back for. Whatever the case, the only way to break habits of negative thinking, is to build new habits of positive thinking.

When it comes to self-esteem, you have to accept that moments of failure and rejection are a part of life, no matter who you are. Every one of us deals with failure. None of us are perfect. But far too often, people think of failure as a purely bad thing, when in fact, failure is simply a human thing. If we think about it differently, we might come to the conclusion that failure can actually be a good thing. Failure can be a great teacher. It is necessary to experience failure in order to grow a thicker skin. Resilience is extremely important in the world we live in. Competition in the workplace is strong. Competition in the dating world is strong too. But the more failures we endure, the stronger we become. We can use failure as a means to decide what's really important to us and what skills we need to improve upon, or we can use it to beat ourselves up and vow to never try anything ever again. Failure is just part of the game. It is not a judgement on YOU. Remember, it is not about how you got knocked down. It's always about how you get back up.

There are a lot of things that may have caused your self-esteem to drop, and uncovering the root of the problem could be useful. If self-esteem has been an issue for you in the long or short term, take some time to think about any events or relationships that may have contributed to it.

Did someone say or do something to you?
Were you rejected by your family or a parent?
Was there a traumatic incident that you never fully recovered from?
Did your parents fail to teach you how to love yourself, or did they withhold their love from you?
Have you been overlooked or underestimated?
Do you have friends who are overly critical of you? A
re there people at work who put you down or don't include you?
Is your self-esteem tied too closely to your love life?
Were you in an abusive or harmful relationship?
Have you been single for a long time?
Have you made poor choices?
Is your partner unsupportive or critical of you?
Are you unhappy with how your life is professionally or educationally?
Is there something you wished you had done?
Is it too late to accomplish it now?

Asking yourself questions like this can be helpful when trying to get to the root of the problem. They can be something to think about when you are meditating or relaxing. Just remember that whenever you indulge in this type of thinking, you don't allow yourself to go too far. These exercises should only be used as a means of discovery. If you notice a serious dip in your mood or you feel very emotionally activated when doing this type of thinking, take a break, talk to someone you trust, and increase your self-care.

Getting your self-esteem back in healthy territory isn't going to be something that happens overnight. But when you get used to offering yourself praise and recognition when you deserve it, your progress will really pick up speed. Positive self-practices will serve you well throughout life, so it's always a good idea move towards being kinder to yourself. A good way to harvest positive feelings for yourself is to set some realistic goals. These can be big goals with many small stepping stones along the way, or smaller goals that you might achieve in just a day or a week.

Accomplishing goals is a great way to boost self-admiration, while solidifying your determination to have a more fulfilling life. Is there anything you wish you had done in the past that you might be able to try for again? Are there any unfinished projects you could finish? What could you do that would prove to yourself that you are capable and worthy? You don't have to put a lot of pressure on yourself with things like this. At this point you are already working on a lot. Remember that every single step you are taking to improve your quality of life is praiseworthy. It takes courage to embark on a period of self-progression. As always, go easy on yourself. Take baby steps if they're easier than long strides. There is no right or wrong way in self progression.

The Power of Change - Lesson 9

Think about any unfinished business that could be detrimental to your self-esteem. Is there someone you need to forgive or bury the hatchet with? Is there someone you need to confront? Have you started something that you really need to finish so that you can move on from it? Is there something or someone that is actively holding you down, and if so, is there something you can do to eradicate that negative force from your life? Remember that everyone deserves a sense of inner peace. If something is getting in the way of yours, make a promise to yourself to deal with it once and for all.

The Key Component of Healthy Relationships

You may be wondering how a section on relationships is relevant to social anxiety. But as I mentioned at the start of this section, when it comes to personal growth, we have to accept that very few of our struggles are completely isolated. Human life is complex. Our identities are intrinsically tied to our experiences as well as our natural born qualities. Our *self* is defined by the many unique experiences each one of us has. No two people have had the same life. We all feel differently and think differently because we have all lived differently. But the thing is, most of who and how we are is connected. So when we embark on a journey of self-development, we have to think of ourselves as whole beings rather than mere vessels of smaller symptoms and unrelated problems.

The fact is, relationships are a massive part of human life. They are relevant to everything we do. This includes our current relationships as well as those we've had in the past. The relationships we had with our primary caregivers when we were small children will naturally affect the way we relate to people for the rest of our lives. An unhealthy relationship with a parent could cause similar relationship patterns to be repeated with friends, lovers, and people of authority. If you have had, or are currently in relationships that are causing you pain, this may very well be linked to both your self-esteem *and* your experience with anxiety. Other people can have an immense amount of power over how we think and feel. What we have to remember and stay true to, is that our relationships with other people should make us feel *good*. They should make us feel good about who we are. They should make us feel lucky and positive about the world we live in.

Relationships will always have a significant impact on our feelings of self-worth, so if we are unsatisfied or unhappy in them, chances are we'll see a decrease in self-esteem and a rise in anxiety. Therefore, relationships that make you feel stressed out, sucked dry, anxious or bad about yourself need to be addressed in the interest of moving forward in life.

Think of people as falling into two categories: drains and radiators. In life, we have to stay close to the radiators; those people who are warm, who make us feel good about ourselves and the world around us, who make us laugh and feel united. And of course, we need to move away from the drains; those people who leave us feeling empty and negative, who make us feel resentful or apathetic, who zap our energy and rob us of positivity. I know that it can seem reductive to put everyone in your life into two categories, and of course there are exceptions.

For instance, there are plenty of radiators in the world who temporarily turn into drains when they're experiencing hard times. For people like this, you might have to be the radiator for them until they get back on their feet. So I am not proposing that you end all the relationships you have if they're just stuck in a rut. Rather, I hope to compel you to think more about how much time you spend with the people in your life, and how they are affecting you. Are you spending more time with the drains than the radiators? If so, taking some steps to rebalance that could mean lifting your own mood. Is there a drain in your life who is taking up way too much of your time and energy? If so, it may be time to set some boundaries. Is there someone that makes you feel great about yourself and who always makes you smile? If so, prioritize that relationship.

A good rule to live by is that after spending time with someone, you should both leave with the same amount of emotional energy you started with, or more. If you regularly leave someone feeling drained, or you notice that someone else is feeling drained by you, something needs to change.

Our friends are some of the most important people in our lives. For many, our friends are our chosen families. So it's important to value our friendships and keep them in healthy territory. A healthy friendship will always be mutually beneficial. One of you should not be charge of always caring for the other. It should be equal and even. When one friend is down, the other will lift them up. But if one person is always down and the other is forced to do all the heavy lifting, the relationship has become unbalanced. Healthy friendships should make you feel good. They should be trusting and honest. Mutual respect is extremely important in friendships. It is not necessary for you and your friends to have all the same interests, but it is necessary that you both respect each other's interests. A good friend will always be open and honest. They will tell you when you're going off track and big you up when you're doing well.

Romantic relationships are similar in that they should also be mutually beneficial, respectful, and balanced. Someone who truly loves you should be good to you and good for you. They should lift you up, not put you down. They should want the best for you rather than feeling jealous when you succeed. A good romantic partner is trustworthy and kind. They will not betray or purposefully hurt you. You should feel valued and respected in your relationship. If some or many of these basic traits are missing, you may need to think more about the health of your relationship. If you regularly feel sad, beaten down, unsatisfied, or disrespected in your relationship, something may be wrong. Relationships may deteriorate over time. This doesn't always mean the end is near, but it may mean that a little TLC is needed to get things back on track.

If your relationship is clearly and obviously adding to feelings of low self-worth or increasing your struggles with social anxiety, you may need to have some difficult conversations. You may need to make some changes or take some risks. These are not easy things to talk about, but the way we are treated by others is a very important part of our lives. It's okay to assess things once in a while and make adjustments where needed. Remember too that when you assess your relationships, you have to be honest with yourself about the effect you are having on others as well. None of us are victims all the time. Usually there are a few things we could be doing better too, things we need to be mindful of in the future. Life is a learning process. We all make mistakes and learn lessons the hard way sometimes. It can be a painful process, but it can also be a part of better things to come.

If you have any relationship patterns that you know are harmful to you, such as having been in one or more abusive relationships, you might want to consider looking into this with a therapist or counsellor. Relationship patterns can be very hard to break but there are things you can do to make the process easier. Having an impartial, realistic, helpful person on your side can make a huge difference. Having had multiple abusive or harmful relationships can make one more likely to experience similar problems in the future. Unhealthy relationships are too hard on us to ignore. Part of taking good care of ourselves is making sure that we protect ourselves from harmful people, so if this is something you need to address, try to take it seriously. I know that it can be extremely frightening to deal with these things head on, so consider talking to someone who you trust and avail of any good advice you receive.

If poor relationships with your family are linked to your feelings of anxiety or any issues with your self-esteem, you may need to address these too. Difficulties with family members are extremely common and are among the most painful experiences any of us can have. Being abused or neglected in childhood can have dramatic effects on how we view ourselves; often leading to feeling inferior in relationships or repeating patterns of neglect and abuse. It's rarely pleasant to have difficult conversations with your family, but if you've been made to feel like the underdog or the black sheep your whole life, you may need to express this to your family members. You may need to stand up for yourself now. If you've been taken advantage of or overlooked by your family, this may need to be addressed. If your family fail to show you respect or treat you with dignity, something needs to change. Families are complex and familial guilt can be a powerful force. Sometimes there will be things we will never be able to change. But thinking about these things with a counsellor may help if you don't feel like you can confront your family members about them directly.

Remember that people who have had difficult pasts need to learn to express even more self-love than other people. We may be more sensitive or slightly emotionally immature because of the hardships we've endured. As such, we have to praise ourselves more, recognize our strong suits more often, and use self-care to lift ourselves up on a regular basis. We have to express self-forgiveness. We might not be able to change how people have treated us, but we can always change how we treat ourselves. Learning to be kind to yourself may be the most important lesson you ever learn. So make sure that you value yourself enough to fine tune the relationships in your life. Make sure you're getting what you need out of your relationships. Make sure that you are not letting yourself be harmed in any way.

Your New Life. Well Wishes From The Author

I sincerely hope that you have found solace and inspiration in this book. Social anxiety is common in the world we live in. It is not a sign that something is inherently wrong with you. It is not a sign that you have been broken nor defeated. Life is rarely all good or all bad. It ebbs and flows, goes up and down. Living through difficult times is just a part of life. No one is exempt from pain and troubles. But remember that life is long. Even if you've lived for 50 years feeling riddled with anxiety the entire time, you could still have another 50 ahead of you that are completely anxiety-free. The important thing is that you always hold onto hope. Do not cling to your struggles. Don't let them define you or become part of your identity. You can overcome any obstacle. Some will be simple hurdles, others will be marathons, but none of them will be permanent. Hold onto that hope for dear life. Believe in yourself and the possibility of a truly fulfilling future.

Forgive yourself if you had to take a little detour on the way to success. Some of the best people are late bloomers. Accept that everything you have been through up to now has made you the person you are today. The kind of person who cares so much about their own quality of life that they are dedicated to becoming an even better version of who they are. Recognize your strengths, live up to your values, give yourself room to make some mistakes. You are only human. Don't place unrealistic expectations or harsh judgements on yourself anymore. There is only one person you have to live with your entire life and that person is you. So keep investing in that person. Keep loving them and feeding them. Keep challenging them and rooting for them.

I'd like to wish you all the very best in the rest of your journey. I hope that self-development will be something you continue to embark on for years to come. We all have an immense capacity for learning. We can all grow and change no matter how old we are or what we've been through. There can always be better times ahead. So please don't give up now, the journey has just begun.